This book is dedicated to my children for being in this world, giving me hope for the next generation.

The Rise Of Advanced Thought: How To Train Your Thinking To Achieve Almost Anything

By Jonathan MacDonald

Foreword by Ed O'Grady, Head of Psychology, The Beauchamp College, Leicester

Introduction

Section One: The World's Least Understood Muscle

Chapter 1: From Coin Flip to Mind Flip

Chapter 2: From Mind Flips to Mind Flops and How to Diagnose Them
- The Thought Assessment Framework

Chapter 3: The Influenced
- The Ambiguity Effect
- Anchoring/Focalism
- An Availability Cascade
- The Mere-Exposure Effect
- Attentional Bias
- The Availability Heuristic
- The Bandwagon Effect
- Salience Bias
- Groupthink

Chapter 4: The Certain
- Choice-supportive Bias
- Belief Bias
- Confirmation Bias
- Illusory Correlation
- Escalation of Commitment
- Status Quo Bias

- The Ostrich Effect
- Not Invented Here

Chapter 5: The Gambler
- Hyperbolic Discounting
- Neglect of Probability
- Normalcy Bias
- Optimism Bias
- The Gambler's Fallacy

Chapter 6: The Inward
- False-Consensus Effect
- A Self-Serving Bias
- The Pseudocertainty Effect
- The Halo Effect
- Argumentative Theory of Reasoning
- The Observer-Expectancy Effect
- The Bias Blind Spot

Section Two: Understanding and Training our Thought Muscle

Chapter 7: The Five Qualities of the Thought Muscle
- Clarity of Response
- A Strength to Persist
- A Recognition of the Likely Impact of Actions
- A Flexibility of Thought
- True Alignment with Personal or Corporate Values

Chapter 8: Mind Flip 1: Developing a Clarity of Response
- Taking a Pause for Reflection
- Developing a Clear Focus
- Making a Mindful Choice
- The Clarity of Response Workout

Chapter 9: Mind Flip 2: Building Our Strength to Persist
- Itemizing the Challenge
- Grasping the Opportunity

- Reframing The Target
- The Strength to Persist Workout

Chapter 10: Mind Flip 3: Becoming Obsessed with Impact
- The Impact Workout: The Seven Steps of Positively Impacting Your Goals
- Visualize the Activity, Event, or Result that you Desire
- Create Visual Imagery Connected to your Goal
- Consider the Actual Chain of Events Needed to Achieve Your Goal
- Start to Move Your Visualization into the Real World Around You
- Create a Selection of Affirmative Phrases to Motivate Yourself
- Imagine Yourself Overcoming Setbacks
- Return Every Week to your Original Vision

Chapter 11: Mind Flip 4: Gaining Flexibility to Achieve Your Goals
- Elevating Our Core Purpose
- Speculating to Gain Evidence Through Experimentation
- The Flexibility Workout: The Five Steps To Making Your Thought Processes Flexible

Chapter 12: Mind Flip 5: Aligning Decisions with Core Values
- The Aligning Decisions with Core Values Workout

Conclusion
- Five Limits
- Truth In Our Time
- Final Words

Appendix: My Coins Flips - A Painful Yet Rewarding History

Foreword by Ed O'Grady. Head of The Beauchamp College, Leicester

I am a boulderer: a follower and active practitioner of a style of climbing characterised by technical, usually powerful problems, up to about four or five meters high. Without ropes. My typical climbing scenario is that I have to reach for a hold, but this is the scary, crux move. I have seen good climbers (better than me), fall off and heard others say how bad the hold is. I stretch up to reach, but all the elasticity seems to have gone from my body. It does not want to stretch. It feels like various bits of my body are arguing about the appropriate course of action. The question is which bit is going to win?

"Come on, you can do this!" I hear most bits of my body saying.
"No, I cannot!" says my head. "It is too high and too far. I am going to fall and die!"

I bail and jump off. We do have crash mats, but they look very small and far away all of a sudden when you are way above them.

In real, grown-up life, my work is as head of psychology at The Beauchamp College in Leicester. This gives me a certain insight into the scenario described above. The reality is that, as I try to stretch up, my feet are solidly planted with no concern for their security. I am not going to fall any further than the height I am currently very (well, relatively) happy at. The only thing getting higher is my head, which remains connected in the same way it always was to my feet. So, my head, with nothing to go on except its own worries, paranoia and biases, wins the argument.

Over the years, I have discovered that my body is capable of much more than I may have given it credit for. The thing that holds me back is my head. All too often, its inability to properly assess the reality of a situation, correctly frame its perceptions and select the appropriate schema to help direct the processing of current inputs, is the thing restricting progress and growth. As a psychologist with a particular interest in the role of mindset and irrational decision-making, I know how ridiculous my thinking is. This is both a blessing and a curse!

I have climbed higher; I have climbed harder, I have seen other people like me, climb it! I just need to find my superpower by adjusting the way I think.

I first met Jonathan several years ago at a TEDx event and thought that he was the most effective speaker that I had ever seen. I was lucky in persuading him to come to present at a student conference at my own college. Just watching Jonathan prepare for his presentation showed me that there was a man with incredible attention to detail. He was making subtle changes to his presentation to optimize it for the precise nature of the audience. The importance of the clarity of the message was paramount and I have discovered this is central to his approach in all his work.

That event led to a wonderful collaboration in which we were able to put into practice Jonathan's expertise in the psychology of decision-making, behaviour modification and the aspect of his work that fascinated me most, cognitive bias.

I am tempted to say that what he does is simple, but that would be unfair (and far too simplistic). In reality, it is fundamental: basic in the way that musical scales are basic or the way in which beginners' techniques in martial arts are basic. They are essential in providing a solid foundation for everything else, taking years of training and refinement. The one thing they are not is simple. Jonathan is able to apply years of careful study and practical application in understanding the cognitive biases people put up to the communications addressed at them. With an understanding of these barriers, he is able to unpick them through the reframing of communications.

In our case, Jonathan was able to help us understand the ways in which students perceived messages and the biases they put up to communications within the college environment. Then, by re-framing our messaging, bring about subtle changes through norm readjustment that had a positive impact on students.

In the same way that Jonathan has applied this knowledge base and his experience, to help his clients impact on the behaviour of others, now in "The Rise Of Advanced Thought" he challenges us as individuals and organizations, to apply those fundamentals of psychology to ourselves and our businesses.

We are all held back by our heads not wanting to go for that hold, but an understanding of the processes and mechanisms by which we place these artificial restrictions on ourselves, allows us to free ourselves. We can progress, we can reach further, we can find new ways of moving forward, and up.

So why "The Rise Of Advanced Thought"? There are lots of books about growth mindset, positive thinking and personal development and I have read a lot of them. Many of you have probably had the same experience as me. As you read you think "This is amazing!" Everything resonates. You see your own behaviour and decision-making in every illustration and then... nothing. It all becomes a rather vague academic memory, just another bit of accumulated pop psychology knowledge. What you need is a counsellor, an instructor, a consultant. Someone who can take you step-by-step through a process, telling you what to do and more importantly making you do it. Advanced Thought is more than an intellectual consideration, it requires a fundamental assessment and adjustment of our perception of reality.

Secondly, you will find as you start to read that Jonathan not only talks the talk, he walks the walk and fights the fight! Jonathan does not just advise others on how they should think and behave, he has used himself as his own testbed and guinea pig. In my mind, this is the psychological equivalent of Barry Marshall demonstrating the link between helicobacter pylori and stomach ulcers, by testing it on the only human patient that he could ethically justify using:

himself. That might sound like rather a dramatic comparison to make, but once you see the nature of the coin-flip challenges that Jonathan has subjected himself to over the last 14 years, I think you might agree that some of them had possible consequences that would need a lot more than a good dose of antibiotics to sort out.

If your feet are well and truly planted and your head thinks it is moving onward and upward, but in fact, you are getting nowhere; then you need to properly interrogate your mentality, consider your cognitive biases and reframe your thinking. From there, it is a question of moving this reframed thinking towards actual action and real-world behaviour. By engaging with the process outlined in the following chapters and reframing the negative thinking that is restricting your growth or the growth of your organization, you too will be better able to succeed in your own coin-flip challenge and truly unlock the advanced thought within you.

Ed O'Grady, Head of Psychology, The Beauchamp College, Leicester. Author and illustrator: The Evolution of Falling

Introduction:

When I wrote *Powered by Change*, the predecessor to this book, I was aware that the methodologies found within it would resonate with some people more than others. Obviously, I was honoured that the book became a Sunday Times Bestseller, however the real test came from companies applying the tools practically. This was when *Powered by Change* really took flight and now is an extremely powerful online platform for business acceleration (poweredbychange.com). Reading a book is one thing but applying it to the real world and seeing the results, is something quite profound. I'm tremendously excited by the numerous companies and business coaches who use the platform, positively impacting businesses all over the world, every hour of every day.

So, why is there a need for a sequel? Surely *Powered by Change* is 'enough'?

The truth is; to *really* understand and benefit from *Powered by Change*, one needs a *thorough* comprehension of how the human brain approaches decision-making.

Businesses are not inanimate objects, they are collections of humans. A 'business book' is, by default, a book about humans and how humans think and behave.

In addition to addressing the business practices and themes presented in the first book, there needed to be a companion guide to help individuals and organizations to understand and leverage the powers of their minds. I feel duty-bound to provide readers the tools necessary to make the decisions needed to survive and thrive in our perpetually changing world. It would be remiss of me to ignore the pressing requirement to understand how to make, and follow, challenging decisions. With all our worry, fear, regret and remorse, I also feel that us humans suffer from a significant misuse of imagination.

The book you are now reading is as much of a prequel as it is a sequel. You can read either in advance of the other. If you are reading this book first, rest assured that before you arrive at the original *Powered by Change* frameworks of, for example, why a company needs a purpose, how its people run on a belief syntax, how an organization can construct a range of products and how a company can create effectively operating processes; it would be very beneficial to have a heightened awareness of how one can control and develop the brain processes that are going to drive those decisions.

In short, before the four blades of the metaphorical windmill on *Powered by Change's* cover can begin to turn, a deep understanding of human thought infrastructure is very beneficial. That should, I hope, justify the order of this book first. However, the converse is also true. If you have arrived here after the first book, you can now double-down on the metaphorical windmill you have built and, essentially, incorporate that windmill into your mind. This is Advanced Thought, and what this book is all about.

Since the first book in 2018, I have witnessed the need for a book containing a body of understanding that will help individuals and organizations to digest and use *Powered by Change* in the most effective manner. That realisation could only be aimed at enabling the further understanding of the human brain, our most important muscle but one that is neglected in all the gyms around the world.

Everything starts with thought.

We tend to assume that the past is a predictor of our future, *but there is no future other than the one we are building now*. The only future that exists stems from the decisions that we make. Waiting for the future to arrive and then change the way that we think is disingenuous. We have to change the way that we think now in order for our futures to be better. *Powered by Change's* virtual windmill that can weather the winds of perpetual change can only be built if we cast aside the blinkers through which we look at that task. That is the reason why this book had to be written.

The Rise Of Advanced Thought is the fruit of all the effort I went to following the launch and real-world application of *Powered by Change*, researching the science behind how the human thought and decision-making processes work.

I began to dig very deep into how we think. What processes drive our behaviour and how can we understand, influence and change those to drive much better business decisions?

Yes, we need to assemble our windmill, but we also need to assemble our thoughts. Our *internal* windmill.

As a companion to the four blades of the *Powered by Change* windmill, there are five physiological thought muscle qualities that are little understood. Those five thought muscle qualities are:

- Clarity of Response
- A Strength to Persist
- A Recognition of the Likely Impact of Actions
- A Flexibility of Thought
- True Alignment with Personal or Corporate Values

These will be detailed later in the book and comprehending these will enable the thought process to be seen as a way of training a human muscle to perform much more effectively, rather than as an obscure, theoretical piece of neuroscience.

All this should come with a warning. Advanced Thought requires a considerable level of personal accountability. The tools outlined in this book will help in the task that you ask your mind to perform but they are just that: tools. The decisions that you need to make are in your domain and some of them may be difficult to take. Even when you are driving with the aid of a satellite navigation system, it is still necessary to follow the directions. Sometimes, the inertia that I have observed with us manipulating our thoughts and then acting on them is due to us really wanting a "quick fix". Our need for instant gratification has been intensified in a world of digital connectivity, where double-clicking on an internet link can appear to be the easiest solution. In my experience, however, this is rarely the best thought-out option available. Outsourcing our intellect and knowledge in this fashion will limit our effectiveness in the long run, not enhance it.

A huge part of the reason I have written this book is my horror at this developing trend. I have five major concerns, as follows:

1) A Lack of Authenticity

Our digital hyper-connected world is a playground for those who have no requirement for being authentic. It seems that being true to who or what you are is optional in today's world. This apparent option is enabled by the ability to 'hide' behind our screens, whilst casting aspersions and opinion to others. The risk is that personal accountability falls away, and the importance of authenticity and integrity is only remembered as something of generations past.

2) Digital Amnesia

A second concern is what I term "digital amnesia". We open mapping apps even though we know perfectly where a destination is and how to get there. We tell somebody to "just Google it" when they ask a question that we could probably answer satisfactorily. If we downgrade human memory in this fashion, we are under-serving the structure of our neurology, which is based on the many connections that store our past experiences in our brains for later use as reference. So, we are making ourselves dumber by relying on digital devices to be our memory.

3) Anxiety and Decision Fatigue

We appear to be developing a generation of anxiety and decision fatigue. The anxiety stems from fretting whether we are still sufficient or 'enough', comparing ourselves to people we follow on Instagram or Twitter, or to see if we can be "liked" as much as some of our Facebook friends. Decision fatigue in turn is a consequence of having an overload of information that, while often trivial in nature, is viewed by many of us as being imperative to making a wise choice. Thus, we become overwhelmed by decision fatigue and the result is yet more anxiety. The two are intertwined.

4) Reality Dysmorphia

These issues are causing an important problem of reality dysmorphia within society. Our view of reality is increasingly based upon a tiny sliver of information that is massively biased but forms our entire view of what is really going on. It results in us mis-sizing reality by providing a limited view of the world and therefore a limited realization of our opportunities and our potential. It makes us less able to make effective decisions and, without remedial action, it will damage our ability to follow the lessons in this book and the one before, about being adaptable and resilient enough to survive and thrive in a world of perpetual change.

I believe that this reality dysmorphia is a major challenge. Because we are not exploring *what we do not know that we do not know*, we may have even bigger problems than we think. Our ability to handle disruptive technology, find the right talent and secure the best investment opportunities is minimized. We end up minimizing potential and maximizing threats and risks. It means we can not elevate our purpose or come up with new purposes for existing methodologies – something that I describe as 'transposition' in *Powered by Change*. We can not add a porous and flexible framework of processes to our operations and we can not find mess inside markets to fix. These issues limit anything and everything we could have achieved.

5) A Falsehood of Certainty

Paradoxically, these circumstances are resulting in us becoming more "certain" about everything, despite our lack of knowledge. Whether it is dispensing armchair politics over various international changes, or the best way to play against the Germans at soccer, everybody now seems to be a pundit. Psychologists call this the Dunning-Kruger Effect: a phenomenon where a tiny piece of information can lead to a bloated over-confidence. It makes us dangerous to ourselves and in my view needs to be checked. We need to be *less* confident about what we know and much more *curious* about what we do not.

It would be unrealistic of me to suggest, after stating all this, that all the answers to all these complex issues are in this book. However, I do believe that gaining the ability of Advanced Thought will aid us all in this greater human quest.

This book is for people who fundamentally want to achieve more. Please read on and allow me to take you on that journey.

Section One: The World's Least Understood Muscle

Chapter 1: From Coin Flip to Mind Flip

"Time is the coin of your life. It is the only coin you have and only you can determine how it will be spent." – Carl Sandburg

Let us start with a challenge. Make a list right now of five things that you would deem impossible to achieve if you were asked to do so within the next two years. Then list the reasons why these accomplishments would be impossible for you.

Pretty easy, eh? We all have well-defined personal capabilities. The key to progressing in life is surely just to know what they are and to never push the boundaries.

Wrong. Think again using the following extra condition. Have the challenges that you have identified *ever* been achieved by a single human being or organization? If someone else has done it, then you could too. Only if the answer is "no," will your primary objection to yourself achieving it be valid.

Look again at your reasons for resisting the hypothetical challenges. Are they actually real and relevant or are they merely excuses because you do not want to go through the effort, pain and personal sacrifices that go hand in hand with achieving goals that sit outside your comfort zone? The rest is internal bias, negativity and self-limitation.

If that is really how you want to live your life, go right ahead. But the bad news is that our leaders and organizations are stuck in this no-man's land too and that they are making bad decisions as a result. The choices that they could be making, which hold the prospect of enabling deeper insights and addressing the issues that face them with greater wisdom, are not available to them. Why? Because they are obscured by a cloud that cannot be cleared until they realize what they are in fact capable of, if they are prepared to make the sacrifices entailed.

What qualifies me to say this? It is because, in my own small way, I have been making such sacrifices and achieving what I honestly believed was personally impossible. For the past 15 years, I have performed an annual New Year's Eve ritual. Just before midnight, I flip a coin between two resolutions, both of which meet the following basic requirement. They must target a personal goal that I do not in all practicality believe that I am capable of accomplishing. I give myself 24 months to achieve the target chosen by heads or tails and every single year I have achieved them.

The coin flips force me to choose between two options that are theoretically "scary" and in which I have no capability. Despite this dominating thought, this annual exercise has reaped two bronze medals in the world championships of a martial art I had never previously practiced. I have also run a marathon, learnt the German, Dutch, Italian and Portuguese languages from scratch, taught myself to write left-handed and lost 35kg in weight.

My coin flips have also resulted in me tracing and forgiving, face-to-face, the perpetrators of the numerous broken bones that I suffered in my schooldays. Even my previous book *Powered by Change* was the successful result of a coin flip (2016 target: author a Sunday Times Best-selling book).

The idea began on December 31, 2005 at a house party where one of my acquaintances had just run the Marathon-de-Sables, a 90km race across the Sahara Desert. This five-day event, where competitors have to carry on their backs everything they are going to consume and live in over this period is run in blazing temperatures and is one of the most dangerous, gruelling races on the planet.

My friend had just achieved a finish, while I was going through one of the most difficult periods of my professional life, losing almost everything in the collapse of a TV business I'd created. Four years earlier, I had been chairman of the British music industry. Now, my mindset was pretty dark. In May 2004, I had just £12.67 in the bank and of no fixed abode. Nineteen months on, my situation was not much better.

I looked at my acquaintance enviously and wondered how I could also set out to feel a sense of achievement in something more than mere survival because all I was doing at the time was day-to-day graft. Was there something I could set out to achieve, affordably, that would give me a greater enthusiasm for living than just pure survival? I decided at that moment that I would either run a marathon, despite having never run even a mile in my life, or swim the English Channel, despite having never achieved a long-distance open-water swim. The time ticked down to 11.55pm and I picked up a 50 pence piece and announced to friends in the kitchen that I would achieve either of these two targets. The marathon was selected as the tails option, with the swim heads, and as the clock struck midnight, I flipped the coin. It landed on tails and three and a half months later I stood on Greenwich Common at the start line of the 2006 London Marathon with 33,000 other people. Six and a half hours later, I had a ruptured Achilles heel, lost three of my toenails, suffered bleeding nipples and almost had an asthma attack. I walked the last seven miles and felt like I had almost died - *but I did it*.

After that, I swore that I would never do another coin flip, dismissing it as a stupid idea. But a year later, I tossed another coin: the choice was between learning to write left-handed and teaching myself to speak German to a level high enough for native speakers to ask which part of Germany I was from. The German side of the coin came up and I duly received the commendation I was seeking in a pub in Dusseldorf. Since then, I have flipped a coin between two outrageous "personally-unachievable" options at the dawning of every new year.

On the eve of 2018, I flipped a coin between a multi-month silent retreat and getting selected to compete in a world championship, in a martial art I have never practiced before. Seven months later, following 900 hours of training in sports, Brazilian and traditional Jiu Jitsu – none of which I had ever previously performed, I arrived at the British National Sports Jiu Jitsu Championships, where the world championships squad is selected. In the heavyweight final I fought an extremely experienced Black Belt and defeated him in under a minute. I was selected to the world championships and relatively soon decided to stop the process, after all, the coin flip was to get selected to the world's, not anything more.

Another five months went by and on New Year's Eve 2018 I flipped a coin between competing at the Jiu-Jitsu world championships and climbing the vertical cliff face of El Capitan in California's Yosemite National Park without ropes. Perhaps fortuitously, since I have never climbed more than a ladder and am not a fan of heights, the coin landed on heads and I called the squad captain who I had previously told I would not be continuing. "*I am in*," I announced. The hard-core training began the very next day and we flew to Orlando, Florida at the beginning of August 2019 to fight for Great Britain on the world stage.

The route to the world championships was the most physically demanding coin flip I had ever achieved but taking that a stage further and fighting for my country in my newly acquired sport against 200 competitors in Orlando took me to a new, heightened point of difficulty. I had never known the life of elite-level world athletes. In Jiu-Jitsu, your entire life gets configured around what will possibly come down to three minutes, but it is not about technique or even physical stamina. What I now realize is that medallists in world championships are mindset experts. They are actually winning medals with their minds and I was in a room of medallists.

Fighting as a middleweight after losing 10kg, I was told by my coach to take a bye on the first day of competition, allowing a fellow team member to graduate up the ranks on that day. I did so and this team member went on to win gold in the Masters (over-40s) section. On the second day, for competitors of any age, I was drawn against the reigning world champion, American James Kyujin, who had not lost a fight for more than a decade. He beat me by one point. I won my other fights to get into silver position and then in the final fight the competitor I was fighting carried out an illegal move that the referees did not see. Just before my ankle was about to snap, I tapped out, retiring from the contest and stopping the fight. My opponent therefore won silver and I was awarded bronze. So, within 18 months of taking up the sport, I ranked third in the world at it. On the third day of the event, I competed against James Kyujin again and lost again, this time by three points. I won all my other fights but so did the Australian team, so a coin was flipped to decide second and third place. Yes, the irony wasn't lost on me! Britain lost the flip, so I received another bronze. This remains the only coin flip that I have ever lost, though I did of course win my own coin flip. I also suffered hairline fractures of a knuckle and my right elbow and a ruptured hamstring in my right leg. That hurt, though the damage was much worse in the 2018 British Championships when I fractured my fifth metacarpal and suffered a broken rib.

Achieving the 2019 coin flip goal took every single ounce of my mental processing ability and physical effort, training between ten and 14 times a week in locations ranging from Yorkshire to Hampshire and completing Army circuits. I eschewed normal eating, drinking and sleeping habits, more or less giving up alcohol and monitoring everything I consumed, and every unit of energy burnt.

Every coin flip has had its unique challenges, but the most emotionally demanding was my 2010 pledge to forgive to their face, if possible, every person that had ever mistreated or bullied me. I really did not want to do it and I was almost begging for the coin to favour the alternative option, which was to spend four months on a Tibetan monastery retreat, consuming only rice and water and meditating for 12 hours a day in total silence. That would have been much easier.

The forgiveness quest took me 20 months to accomplish. I identified 25 people and was able to find all but two of them. The most profound moment was meeting Richard, who stabbed me through my stomach with a barbecue fork when I was 16 and in the last year of secondary school. He was in the swimming pool with his children when I first located him and refused to speak to me. Six months later, I found him online, explained what I was forgiving him for, and he agreed to meet me on his own. When we met, he said he could not remember the incident as he often got into fights at school. I was simply one of those meaningless incidents. This revelation had a profound impact on me. It may seem bizarre but, initially, I was gutted that I had not been special or chosen; I was simply one of many victims.

Once I had managed to drag myself out of this victim mode, I chatted further with Richard and found that he was a changed man. Within two hours, we had hatched a plan for him to go back and apologise to everyone that he had ever bullied. I helped find him nearly 100 such people and he was good to his word and personally apologized to them all. This experience has had an enormous impact on both Richard and me, and we remain in contact today.

For me, this represented an important personal closure of a seminal period of my life where my experiences colored my entire attitude to life. As I wrote of the bullying in *Powered by Change*:

"Nothing I did seemed to be able to stop it, and I seeped into a mindset that this was what my life was always going to be like, and I couldn't do much about it."

The effort required to track back to one of the hardest experiences of my life and see it from a new perspective made it my hardest coin flip achievement ever and by far the most liberating.

For 2020, I took the coin flip idea even further, outsourcing the choice of candidates for the toss to my followers on Twitter, Instagram, Facebook and LinkedIn. I produced the following four options; learning how to do the splits, starting a degree in Neuroscience within the next three years, losing 10kg in weight and maintaining the loss for three years and re-learning my Portuguese. My followers selected splits as heads and neuroscience as tails. The coin flip landed on tails, but at that moment I decided to set myself the additional challenges of achieving the splits *and* weight loss objectives. As with my methodology for realizing my past targets, I immediately went online, sourcing the necessary resources and expertise. Upon reflection, I widened my annual challenges because they were getting too easy. When you know what is possible for you to achieve, you are spoilt for choice with potential accomplishments.

Openly declaring such annual goals online makes one vulnerable to amateur correction or "fake expertise". Pictures of me training for my splits challenge, for example, were met with instant responses informing me that I was going about the exercise all wrong. There has also been ridicule, even derision. But for me, the annual coin flips are a wonderful yearly reminder of the power that every one of us possesses within our brain cells.

Achieving such tests of endurance brings for me three waves of response. The first is sheer relief, the second is a slightly delayed sense of achievement and the most profound impact then follows: the realization that I have taken a challenge that I "could not" achieve and somehow achieved it. About six or seven months into every year, I am therefore thinking about what else is there that I honestly do not think I can do that I would like to be the next challenge.

Having begun the annual coin flip exercise at a time when I was professionally, personally and emotionally close to rock bottom, the mindset of considering something that I "cannot" do has become core to the experience. When you have nothing, everything seems impossible; all the options appear equally unlikely. Starting with such as approach, has inculcated in me such an attitude that I have come to regard the words "can not" or "impossible" as an enemy. I do find it very difficult to handle somebody saying that a certain event or outcome simply "can not" happen.

Recently, while I was carrying out Army circuits training, a man next to me was really struggling. "I don't actually think that I can do this," he told me as he pulled up. Quietly, I asked him whether anybody anywhere had ever achieved the exercise he was finding so difficult. Of course, it had been achieved; probably many hundreds of thousands of times, he acknowledged. I told my momentary colleague that I could guarantee him that his body was physically able to complete what was needed. All the problems he was encountering at the time were actually due to a mindset issue. Forty minutes later he finished the course.

I have now experienced many situations that are theoretically unachievable but actually possible. I have also found that tasks or challenges that are theoretically unachievable but physically improbable are only the latter because of a mindset.

How have I achieved all this? Not by belonging to some super-human master race but by recognizing at the outset that controlling my mind will enable me to control my actions. That's Advanced Thought. Achieving my coin flip goals relies not upon any great physical attributes that I may or not possess. Instead, I strive to develop five physiological qualities of thought:

- **An Ability to Respond**

My initial reaction when I see the side of the coin that has come up is that I cannot achieve the stated goal. It is just too difficult, and I am just not capable. My first action is then to pause and deliberately disregard that initial mental reaction. I reject it as a re-enaction of what my thought muscle memory would say to itself. I then look at how I can change my negative reactive thought into a positive proactive, productive, responsive one. I examine why my reaction was negative and it has always been so because of a bias that I have used. Specifically, it is usually a status quo bias – a feeling that I am comfortable with the way that things are and have no requirement to change. There is also a Choice-Supportive Bias which sees me use any available evidence to remind myself that I am unable to do something. I regard myself as a world champion in the status quo and Choice-Supportive Bias. However, because I am aware of these fierce biases, I am able to work out how to counter them.

- **Mental Strength**

My second stage is to develop the capability to programme my mind to believe that I am able to achieve a given goal. I find it highly liberating once I can bring myself to believe that the task before me is one of which I am capable. It is effectively turning "I can not" into "I can" and involves looking at why I think I cannot do it and what lessons I can take from that in order to reframe it in my mind. I look at the challenge and consider how I can grow through it. With every single challenge I have set and met, I have looked at where the personal growth opportunity exists. For the forgiveness challenge, for example, not having to carry around a residual victimhood was a wonderful prize which changed how I identify myself and opened up new possibilities for myself. I choose to reframe the way that I think. Achieving every coin flip has involved reframing my thinking to accomplish a change possibility for myself. This gives me purpose and drive. I am not simply trying to achieve the impossible because of a random flip of a coin; I am pursuing it to become an improved version of myself.

- **An Ability to Manage Impacts**

Understanding the link between everything that I think and do and the outcome of those thoughts and actions is vital to ensuring that I achieve the tasks I set out to accomplish. My brain needs to be constantly considering the impact of both what I think and what I do to achieve the desired outcome. Conversely, my mind also has to be crystal-clear about the consequences of potential negative impacts of a stated goal. It is about creating a logical chain of impact events. The optimal coordination of impact occurs when every thought and action is calculated to have the biggest impact. Our thoughts actually create our physical entity because the body does not know the difference between a) an experience and b) a thought about such an experience. Because of this, we have the ability to create a physical impact *just through the way that we think*.

That is Advanced Thought indeed.

The opposite of what I am describing is when I have a goal in mind; my mind has responded, understood what I am trying to achieve and developed the strength to achieve it. But then I carelessly sleepwalk through the activities that will get me to the goal; "accidentally" having an extra slice of cake when trying to lose weight or giving into the temptation to go for a drink when I should be training for a marathon.

It is therefore essential that I monitor how I think to enable the impact to be optimal. Otherwise, I will not be able to achieve the coin flip objective.

The same is true in business. We live in a post-2008 financial crisis world where there is a real and growing demand, particularly among Millennials, for organizations to have clearly set-out corporate visions, missions and purposes. A conventional marketing practice is to verse such intentions in the present so that, rather than referring to something as a target, it is stated as if it had already been achieved.

Take Nike, for example. Its corporate website says: *"Our mission is what drives us to do everything possible to expand human potential. We do that by creating groundbreaking sport innovations, by making our products more sustainably, by building a creative and diverse global team and by making a positive impact in communities where we live and work."*

These are impressive goals, and it is fair to say that the company has credentials behind them. But in order to set these targets and have any realistic prospect of achieving them, Nike's executives had to also consider what circumstances might make their claims seem fatuous, untrue or even embarrassing. In this way, considering potential and actual impacts is an essential part of decision-making.

- **Flexibility of Mindset**

In *Powered by Change*, I asserted that organizations with the ability to "elevate" their thinking so they can identify their core purpose is a key stage (one of the four blades) in developing the ability to respond positively to perpetual change. The same is true of the thought processes needed to achieve great personal transformation or landmarks. Our ability to flexibly experiment to learn more about ourselves. From our individual experiences of the Covid-19 pandemic, many of us may well have been somewhat forced into thinking more flexibly about our work routines, conversations with friends and education for our children. This flexibility can be a very positive part of our personality if we leverage it well.

With the 2016 coin flip about writing a Sunday Times bestseller book, my immediate negative response was that *none* of the tomes that I had previously written had achieved such status. Through a deliberate thought process, I told myself that I was going to *learn* how to write a bestseller. For that to happen, I had to stop my biases creeping in and listen to publishers and experts about what it would take to achieve the objective. The upshot is that I ended up writing a very different book to the one I originally envisaged; but that was the book that ended up accomplishing my goal.

Flexibility of thought involves accepting that one does not need to stick with an initial interpretation. If a certain outcome is the goal, it is that outcome that must be inflexible, not the route of getting there. Flexibility of thought involves creating a new way of thinking about something that will achieve the objective.

In business, this can make the difference between the success and failure, not just of a stated goal, but of the entire organization. Consider the well-documented failures behind the value lost at the likes of records store chain HMV, camera and film-maker Eastman Kodak and mobile giant brand Nokia when the Internet revolution was transforming the business landscape all around them.

As I wrote in *Powered by Change*, HMV's problems stemmed from the fact that its purpose was *"to monetize the physical retail of products. It was wedded to the idea of selling physical products in bricks and mortar stores when all the evidence was that the future was going to be digital, not physical, and sales were going online"*

- **Alignment with Core Values**

Alignment is the quality of thought that enables me to stay alive and content through the biggest challenges that I have ever faced. This is the quality of thought that has taken me longest to develop – for a long time, there were only four. However, after a long struggle with myself, I have realized that if what I am doing is not congruent with what I honestly and sincerely believe in, I become deeply unhappy.

Conversely, if I can find a way of aligning the activities that I do and the thoughts that I have to the values that I hold, then the coin flips become not impossible and unpleasant challenges, but magical moments of personal growth that bookmark stages of my life. I do not choose coin flip challenges in order to align with my values, but I do activate them in alignment with those values.

For example, I saw achieving the Jiu Jitsu challenge as enabling me to be *mindful* of how I was eating and working out and *grateful* to my coaches and competitors. It also let me prioritize my *health*, accept my *inferiority in sport*, enjoy the *adventure* of fighting for my country, develop the *intuition* that martial arts need, evolve into a better human being, and experience the *freedom* of not focusing on the day-to-day grind. Those eight core values enable me to achieve my central value of finding inner *peace*.

Accomplishing that and other coin-flip challenges is an *essential* demonstration of my core being. Not achieving them would have been pointless.

Without these five qualities of thought, there is not a single one of the 14 successful coin flip targets that I have achieved that would have been possible. With them, however, I do not believe that there is a coin flip target that somebody else in the human race has achieved that would actually be impossible for me to accomplish, given the appropriate provision of resources. In short: the achievement of the coin flips is due to the architecture of my *thought patterns*, rather than any natural ability that I may or may not possess.

All my coin flips are detailed in the appendix, and I will return to some of the lessons I have learned through the achievement of these annual targets. What has become clear to me from these rites, however, is this: *everything starts with thought, including our perception of reality.*

The thought qualities I have developed through my coin-flip challenges are highly relevant to the world of business because the decisions that organizations make generate their behaviour and performance. Despite this obvious truth, I have observed a distinct lack of prioritisation about how corporate thinking occurs.

Leaders and companies prioritize their competitive approach, staff culture, product range, office locations, tax structures and shareholder reports but constantly fail to prioritize the deep analysis of what is driving their decisions. Individuals tend to assume that thinking just "happens" when, in fact, our thought-muscle brains need constant stimulation, nurturing and control. Imagine the changes that could be wrought if thinking was generally accepted as a muscle. Executives would spend as much time building its strength as they do flexing their biceps at the gym.

One might respond that this is all about the thinking and strategy work that chief executives conventionally prioritize and indeed there is a veritable library of research papers and books on this subject. Yet very little of this body of knowledge focuses on how people and the groups that they form part of actually think; how their minds physiologically go about making choices, setting targets and seeking to achieve them.

The Physiology of the Brain

Our brain is constructed of about 100 billion neurons. These nerve cells, individual bio-computers with about 60 megabytes (MB) of computer random-access memory (RAM) are interconnected by trillions of synapses which are the connection devices. On average, each one of these trillions of synapses transmits one signal per second, although some send up to 1,000 per second. These transmissions become thoughts and we think around 60,000 to 70,000 of them per day, every day.

Such thoughts can manifest themselves in some people's minds as internal monologues, or conversations with themselves. In the 1930s, Russian psychologist Lev Vygotsky proposed that this was due to external conversations becoming internalized in our brains. Yet, this is not the same for everybody. Some individuals report no such inner monologues, representing thoughts instead as sentences they "hear" or abstract concepts that are initially difficult to convert into words. Whatever process is used by a particular person is often regarded by them as "natural" or their only option. Indeed, they may find it hard to contemplate the possibility of thoughts expressing themselves in other ways.

Dr. Marcus Raichle, a professor of medicine at Washington University School of Medicine in St. Louis, regards the brain as the most expensive energy-consuming organ that humans carry around with them. His research has found that, while the brain represents just 2 per cent of a person's total body weight, it accounts for 20 per cent of the body's energy use. That means during a typical day, a person will burn up about 320 calories just by thinking and – like with traditional muscles - the harder one thinks, the more calories are burned.

Our thinking influences the way we feel and behave. Events and situations that occur in the outside world do not usually cause feelings or behaviour; rather it is an individual's interpretation via thought about those events that will directly lead to feelings and subsequent actions. In some cases, the thoughts we have about a particular situation can be quite unhelpful, and lead to us make decisions that are less likely to have a positive outcome.

Often, the unhelpful thoughts happen so quickly in response to trigger events that we may not even realize what is happening. That is why these thoughts are often referred to as "automatic". These feelings are often a signal that somebody has slipped into automatic pilot and allowed a trigger situation to lead to an unhelpful thought about that situation, which has then resulted in a decision that may be totally unsuitable for the context at that time.

Psychologist Daniel Kahnmann, describes automatic (fast) thinking as "System 1" and deliberate (slow) thinking as "System 2". In his book "Thinking, Fast and Slow," he shows how fast or automatic thinking can lead us to make many mistakes in everyday life. Automatic thinking ("thinking fast") means that we can get on with life for most of the time without too much effort. This helps us make decisions quickly, recognise patterns, fill in gaps in information and carry out well-rehearsed behaviours. Psychologists have also noticed that automatic thoughts can have a direct and really immediate impact on our feelings or emotions, and on our behaviours.

American psychiatrist Dr Aaron T Beck goes further, noticing that negative thinking is a core aspect of depression. Arguing that negative thinking makes people feel depressed and increases the task of recovering from depression, he suggests that thoughts, feelings and behaviours are inter-linked, meaning that changing one of the parts would have an effect on any of the others. As a result, Beck developed a new form of psychotherapy for depression. Rather than focusing on the past, he aimed to use psychotherapy to help tackle depression by changing people's cognitions (or thoughts) and their behaviours. By changing one, or both, of their cognitions or behaviours, Beck proposed that this would also change their emotions, and improve depression. This new therapy was Cognitive Behaviour Therapy, which is today one of the most effective methods of helping people deal with depression.

It may seem strange to focus a personal and corporate development programme on what action can be taken to avoid becoming depressed but addressing the matter in that way can be highly productive.

Later, this book will explain how to develop and pursue such workouts. But first we need to consider the main reasons why people and organizations fail to achieve their goals by making key errors in the ways they make important decisions.

Chapter 2: From Mind Flips to Mind Flops and How to Diagnose Them

"There is nothing either good or bad but thinking makes it so." - Hamlet by William Shakespeare

What I have found fascinating from my decades in business is that the decisions we make as leaders and executives, are often viewed by many stakeholders at the time as being reasonable, rational and considered. However, those very decisions are often being made in alarmingly sub-optimal ways and there is a very high failure rate. According to <u>research conducted by Joep Steffes</u>, a PhD student at Nyenrode Business University in The Netherlands, more than half of all strategic decisions made by directors turn out to be wrong. Steffes blames time constraints, poor information and bias that causes directors to base judgements on biased, limited thoughts, rather than reason or even gut feeling.

"Businesses need to ensure that their directors are making fully-informed decisions by selecting directors based on cognitive capabilities and critical thinking skills," writes Steffes. *"They have to put more cognitive effort into the decision-making process. They need to have decision-governance structures and responsibilities in place that effect how decisions are made and monitor the decision-making process."*

Clayton Christensen, a former professor at Harvard Business School, goes further, finding in his own research, <u>referenced on the Harvard site</u>, that 80 per cent of the 30,000 new products that are launched every year fail as a result of poor decision-making. Christensen's view is that product launches are too focused on customer segmentation, predicting that a certain type of person will be attracted to buy a product. Whereas, he argues, people don't purchase in that way. "*The fact that you're 18 to 35 years old with a college degree does not cause you to buy a product,*" Christensen says. "*It may be correlated with the decision, but it doesn't cause it. We developed this idea because we wanted to understand what *causes us to buy a product, not what's correlated with it. We realized that the causal mechanism behind a purchase is, 'Oh, I've got a job to be done.' And it turns out that it's really effective in allowing a company to build products that people want to buy."* This is contrary to how many executive decisions are made. People prefer predictability, especially when it comes to target market choices. It would be ideal if consumers followed the pattern that executives decide, but it would seem, according to Christensen at least, that this isn't the case.

I suspect this situation is not necessarily fixed in stone. Imagine the wealth that could be generated if this failure rate could be reduced by one-half, one-third or even one-tenth. I fervently believe that such improvements are possible. Why? Because the reason so many decisions end up being mistaken, in hindsight, is that we have not really been thinking clearly at all. Science appears to back this supposition.

As Dr Joe Dispenza discusses in "You Are The Placebo", around 90 per cent of our thoughts are exactly the same as the day before. Thinking the same thoughts leads to the same decisions being made, the same behaviors being demonstrated and largely, the same outcome being realized. We are creatures of habit and we feel comfortable repeating the same patterns each day.

Thoughts are not the only repetitive aspect of our daily routines, the process or method (heuristics) of thinking those thoughts is also a driving factor, as are the biases we apply, mainly without realizing. In the early 1970s, Kahneman alongside fellow psychologist Amos Tversky, started to link heuristics to cognitive biases and from there, the field of research has grown rapidly.

Much of life and business involves making decisions between alternatives that involve risk and probabilities of outcomes that are uncertain. In cognitive psychology this is known as Prospect Theory. The theory states that people make decisions based on the potential value of losses and gains rather than the final outcome, and that people evaluate these losses and gains using some heuristics. The model is descriptive: it tries to model real-life choices, rather than optimal decisions, as normative models do.

Kahneman and Tversky developed Prospect Theory in 1979 and developed it further in 1992 as a psychologically more accurate description of decision-making, compared to the expected utility theory, the appraisal of something based on its value or usefulness. Within Prospect Theory and in wider contexts of heuristics and biases, there are hundreds of patterns or biases that model our thoughts to generate decisions.

The Thought Assessment Framework

Driven by a personal, deep interest into this area, I have spent some time developing a way of assessing thought patterns to highlight what heuristics and biases are at play. This is called the Thought Assessment Framework and it works in the following way:

Below appears a relatively straightforward questionnaire with multiple choice answers. Each question is designed to trigger certain thought patterns and when you are answering the questions, try and do so as instinctively as possible. The more time you spend answering them, the more time you are able to second-guess the answer. As with so many question and answer scenarios, it is tempting to try and guess what the "right" or "most desirable" answer might be. However, in the Thought Assessment Framework, every answer is as valid as any other. Your answers may indicate certain tendencies towards specific biases.

To take part, go to this link online: tinyurl.com/thoughtassessment

You can either read through the below questions in advance of completing the assessment online – or you can go ahead and get the results online first, before reading the remainder of this section. Either way, the tendencies we may be showing are useful indicators of how we may be making decisions, including how we process the information within this book. All of us have various biases and they should not be viewed as being a bad thing.

Again, visit tinyurl.com/thoughtassessment and complete the assessment to get your results. Here is the assessment in case you want to check it out first:

1) A new opportunity has been offered to you, but it isn't something you've explored previously. How do you feel about it?

a) Unless there is really compelling evidence to convince me, I will probably avoid it.

b) I will see if there are any similarities between what I have known from before and this new idea.

c) I am excited by new ideas, regardless of whether they are within my area of knowledge.

d) I will ask my peers/colleagues/mentors/partners to seek advice and gain their opinion.

2) When was the last time you took a significant amount of time to test your assumptions that you tend to rely on in decision-making, to see whether they are still valid?

a) I cannot recall.

b) Fairly often.

c) I do not have assumptions.

d) I regularly test whether my assumptions are valid.

3) How often do you find yourself getting distracted by new and seemingly exciting things, but then lose interest after a relatively short time?

a) All the time.

b) I am not distracted by much.

c) It happens occasionally.

d) I probably do it more than I realize.

4) How do you tend to assess what you believe in?

a) I do not need to assess my beliefs; I just know them to be true.

b) I cross-match things I believe in with evidence I can access.

c) I tend to instinctively know what is true or not.

d) I do not have a particular process.

5) Think of a recent major decision you made. How did you prioritize the information you used to assess your options?

a) I just acted upon instinct.

b) I naturally prioritize things without realizing.

c) I rely on what I have most recently thought.

d) I do not prioritize information. I see all data as equally balanced and worthy.

6) How much influence on my preferences comes from what I am familiar with?

a) None. My preferences are unlinked to what I find familiar.

b) A huge amount. I create my preferences based on what I find most familiar.

c) Not a huge influence because I am continually curious to explore new things to widen my preferences.

d) I am curious to discover more things in life, but I tend to revert back to what I find familiar.

7) How regularly do the actions of someone you compare yourself to, motivate you to follow their lead?

a) Not at all. I think totally independently.

b) I am guided by other people's actions a lot.

c) Not very much, but occasionally it happens.

d) I think it is a good thing to be a follower rather than a leader in most cases.

8) If the answer to a question is unremarkable, boring or tedious, what does your response tend to be?

a) I would prefer to seek an answer that is more interesting, but I will accept whatever the answer is.

b) I do not mind what the answer is, provided that it is the best one possible.

c) I tend to focus on answers that are more striking and unusual.

d) I disregard answers that do not excite me in some way.

9) When you are in a situation with a group of people, how much of your decision-making is based on not wishing to cause conflict?

a) Never. I do not consider conflict (or the avoidance of it) when making decisions.

b) Sometimes. It depends on what we are trying to achieve.

c) Often. I think conflict within a group of people should be avoided at all costs, even at the expense of progress.

d) Conflict is not productive but if it is the cost of progress then so be it.

10) How often do you challenge your preferences by forming a contrary argument that represents the opposite or different point of view?

a) All the time. That is the way I make decisions.

b) I do not need to challenge my preferences.

c) I try to maintain a balance but could do more.

d) I would like to do this more, but I am not sure how.

11) How rational do you consider yourself to be?

a) Highly rational. I take everything into account reasonably and seldom let my own pre-existing beliefs colour my decision-making.

b) Quite rational. I try to be as balanced as possible.

c) Not very rational, I already know what I need to know and do not need to consider other elements.

d) I can be as rational as needed, depending on the circumstances.

12) How do you ensure that you are not preferring something just because it supports what you already believe?

a) Quite the opposite. I always prefer things that support choices I have already made.

b) I always test what I think I prefer to ensure that it is not a previous choice that is biasing me.

c) When I am conscious of it, I try and maintain a rational process of decision-making.

d) I am aware I make decisions based on past choices, but I am not sure how to address this.

13) When you spot a correlation between things, how much do you test to see if they are actually random?

a) Always – I am sceptical of a correlation until I can prove that it is definitely there.

b) Sometimes. I try and ensure a rational view of things that appear correlated.

c) Never. If I have spotted a correlation, then there tends to genuinely be one. I do not need to test it.

d) It has never occurred to me that things that seem correlated may not actually be so.

14) How do you avoid continuing to invest more money, time or energy into something, even when the outcomes are increasingly negative?

a) I can stop investing money, time and energy instantly, as soon as I realize that the outcome is becoming more negative.

b) It is tough to break the cycle as I feel committed to continuing down the path that has been agreed to.

c) I try to maintain a balanced view but tend to keep going a bit longer than I should.

d) I do this quite often. It is something that I am aware of.

15) When a new concept is introduced to you, what tends to be your most immediate reaction?

a) I prefer to stick with what I know.

b) I am really curious about new approaches, even if they have not been tested before.

c) It depends on the concept. A low-risk concept is more likely to be tried than others.

d) Ideally, I would like to try new things, but that is not realistic in some cases.

16) What level of honesty and transparency do you prefer to experience?

a) I want (and provide) 100 per cent honesty and transparency, regardless of whether that is good or bad.

b) There are certain times when total honesty and transparency could cause bad outcomes, so it varies.

c) It depends on the level of importance. You can not be totally honest and transparent the whole time.

d) I do not believe that 100 per cent honesty and transparency is a good thing.

17) If someone else develops something that you would find really useful, despite you having spent time yourself trying to develop something similar, what would your response be?

a) I would continue developing something myself, I would prefer it that way.

b) I do not have a preference as to who develops what, I am more interested in the overall outcome.

c) My competitive advantage is based on ownership, so I would prefer to develop things in-house.

d) I would prefer someone else to develop something that I can then use. It is better that way.

18) If you were offered a smaller reward now, rather than a larger reward much later, what decision would you make?

a) I would probably go for the smaller reward now rather than wait. Who knows what could happen in the meantime?

b) I tend to wait for the larger reward. It is almost always worth it.

c) The larger and later reward would have to be massive for me to wait. So, unless that is the case, I will take what I can now.

d) It totally depends. I do not have one particular view on this unless I know the exact value of both rewards.

19) When you consider the probability of something happening, what is your approach?

a) I weigh up everything, seek out information that I may not have known and finally make a decision on the level of probability.

b) I tend to instinctively sense what the likelihood is.

c) I try to be as fully informed as possible.

d) I do not have a particular approach.

20) How prepared are you for a "worst-case" scenario?

a) I spend a lot of time planning for what could go wrong.

b) I tend to go with the flow and take things as they come.

c) I always have a backup plan so even if things go wrong, I feel that I am pretty well-covered.

d) I do not see the need to prepare for "worst-case" scenarios.

21) How likely do you feel you are to experience a negative event?

a) I am pretty fortunate, so I think that this is fairly unlikely.

b) Life is often a challenge, so I think that there is a fair chance of experiencing a negative event at any stage.

c) I try to stay positive and assume that the best will happen.

d) I do not mind what the chances are, because it is more about how I choose to respond to what happens.

22) How deeply do you investigate the correlation between something happening because something happened before?

a) I have never considered this to be something to investigate.

b) I often see correlation between the past, present and future. I do not need to investigate it much.

c) I often see correlation between the past, present and future but I investigate that correlation to ensure it is accurate.

d) I do not see very much correlation between the past, present and future.

23) In general, do you think most people around you are in agreement with you?

a) Yes. My views are mostly agreed with.

b) Sometimes. It varies, depending on the context.

c) No. I tend to have opinions that most people do not agree with.

d) I do not tend to think about whether people agree with me or not.

24) When things go right or wrong, who tends to be responsible for it?

a) When things go wrong, they tend to be because of factors outside of my control.

b) When things go right, they tend to be because I have enabled them to happen.

c) Mostly, good and bad things tend to be caused by how I have thought or behaved.

d) I do not monitor who is responsible for good and bad things happening.

25) Are you ever truly certain about anything?

a) When I am certain about things. I tend to check my certainty with other people.

b) I am certain about some things and I know them to be true.

c) I am certain about a lot of things, as I have experienced and observed a lot of things in my life.

d) I am not certain about anything.

26) If you see someone you find attractive promoting something, do you tend to think more positively about the product or service?

a) Absolutely. If they endorse it, it is likely to be good.

b) It makes no difference to me; I will make my decision based purely on the quality of what is being promoted.

c) Not often but I would probably spend more attention to the product or service than I usually would.

d) I am against all kinds of marketing so it would actually be a turn-off.

27) When you argue, what do you feel your primary objective is?

a) I need to be seen as being right.

b) I see arguments more like conversations to gain deeper understanding.

c) I try and avoid arguments as much as possible.

d) It depends on the circumstance.

28) When you ask questions of other people, how much influence on their response (or your interpretation of their response) do you think you have?

a) I do not have any influence on others when I ask questions of them and I view responses agnostically.

b) I am aware that how I ask questions may lead people into responding a certain way, so I take that into account when I consider their responses.

c) I have never considered this before.

d) I am aware of this happening and it is actually a useful way of getting the right information.

29) How biased are you in comparison to other people?

a) I can easily observe biases that other people have, and they frustrate me.

b) I am fully aware of the biases I have but others seem not to be so aware.

c) I am curious to understand my biases more. I think we all have them.

d) I do not notice other people's biases.

Assuming you have completed the assessment (tinyurl.com/thoughtassessment), congratulations!

If you have noted down which heuristics and biases you seem to relate to most, you may find there is a pattern, or a grouping. Indeed, bias characteristics can be more similar to some than others. Over time, I have realized that there are four profile groups exist in this regard. Individuals may be more in one than another, but sometimes people may score highly in two main profile groups. Either way, the main thing is to recognise tendencies and work to address any that are not serving the best possible outcome for us.

1: The Influenced

People in this group tend to be highly influenced by factors that may or may not be obvious. The dominant risk for this group is coercion because, if an influencer knew the tendencies of those within it, there may be room for exploitation.

Members of this group are particularly subject to the following biases:

• The Ambiguity Effect

- Anchoring/Focalism
- An Availability Cascade
- The Mere-Exposure Effect
- Attentional Bias
- The Availability Heuristic
- The Bandwagon Effect
- Salience Bias
- Groupthink

2: The Certain

People in this group tend to try and remain in a comfort zone as much as possible. Change is not seen as being very positive. The dominant risk for this group is that change is the only thing that is predictably constant.

Members of this group are particularly subject to the following biases:

- Choice-supportive bias
- Belief Bias
- Confirmation Bias
- Illusory Correlation
- Escalation of Commitment
- Status Quo Bias
- The Ostrich Effect
- Not Invented Here

3: The Gambler

People in this group tend to weigh up chances and place "bets," literally or figuratively, on various levels of outcome predictability. The dominant risk for this group appears in contexts where the level of rationality in decision-making is relatively low.

Members of this group are particularly subject to the following biases:

- Hyperbolic Discounting
- Neglect of Probability
- Normalcy Bias
- Optimism Bias
- The Gambler's Fallacy

4: The Inward

People in this group tend to be relatively introspective and focused on an agenda driven from within. The dominant risk for this group is essentially "self-talk" which may not always generate the best possible decisions.

Members of this group are particularly subject to the following biases:

- False-Consensus Effect
- A Self-Serving Bias
- The Pseudocertainty Effect
- The Halo Effect
- Argumentative Theory of Reasoning
- The Observer-Expectancy Effect
- The Bias Blind Spot

In the following four chapters, I will explain each bias and suggest how it can be understood and countered in order for genuinely better decisions to be made.

You will need to get the results of your Thought Assessment Framework at https://tinyurl.com/thoughtassessment before proceeding any further.

Chapter 3: The Influenced

"Because To influence a person is to give him one's own soul. He does not think his natural thoughts or burn with his natural passions. His virtues are not real to him"- The Picture of Dorian Gray by Oscar Wilde

People belonging to "The Influenced" collection of individuals have a tendency to be highly influenced by factors that may or may not be obvious. This brings a possible danger of constituents being vulnerable to being unduly influenced, or even forced to do something, if someone wanting to control their decision figures out their characteristics.

Those who fall within this group are particularly subject to the following biases:

The Ambiguity Effect

Question 1 is in relation to the Ambiguity Effect. This is where decision-making is affected by a lack of information. So often in business, as in life, a decision needs to be made but evidence is scarce. The effect takes place where people tend to go for the options for which the probability of a favorable outcome is *known*, over an option for which the probability of a favorable outcome is *unknown*.

Answers "a" and "b" are more linked to the ambiguity effect than the other two. One potential way of addressing this is to pause before deciding and create a scenario of the lesser known path. Then, try and experiment with how it might feel if it produced a favorable outcome. Even though it may be less probable, would the result be far greater? This type of scenario planning can reduce the risk of the ambiguity effect and can produce better results than expected.

Anchoring/Focalism

Question 2 is about something called Anchoring, also known as Focalism. This is where an individual relies too heavily on an initial piece of information offered (considered to be the "anchor") when making decisions. This could be a previous research document or something a director has stated in an earlier meeting. Actually, it could be something even more trivial such as a sentence overheard on a train. When this bias is in effect, the type of anchor is less relevant than the fact there is an anchor that forces the reliance of it.

Answers "a" and "c" are fairly good indicators of this bias being at play. One way of addressing this is to note down the top 5 or so factors you are thinking about and place them in order of what you consider to be of importance. Are they justified to be in that order?

Attentional Bias

Question 3 relates to attentional bias. This is the tendency for people's perception to be affected by their recurring thoughts at the time. One popular example is when executives arrive at airports, pick up the most recent best-selling business book, read the back cover and then use that as the main point for the remainder of the week's business meetings. Attentional biases may explain an individual's failure to consider alternative possibilities, as specific thoughts guide the train of thought in a certain manner.

It should come as no surprise that answers "a" and "d" are good indicators of this. One useful method to address it is to ask oneself, if I could only give 25 per cent of my attention to this one particular thing, what would the other 75 per cent of attention be used for?

An Availability Cascade

Question 4 introduces the concept of an Availability Cascade which is a self-reinforcing cycle that explains the development of certain kinds of collective beliefs. This is one that emergent "Thought Leaders" can exploit. The introduction of a novel idea or insight, usually one that seems to explain a complex process in a simple or straightforward manner, gains rapid currency in the popular discourse by its very simplicity and by its apparent insightfulness. This is how memes are created and company slogans are brought to life. We should watch out for this, not only because there is a risk of misinformation, but also because, as Dresden James once wrote: "When a well-packaged web of lies has been sold gradually to the masses over generations, the truth will seem utterly preposterous and its speaker a raving lunatic."

Answer "a" is the primary indicator of this bias, but arguably answers "c" and "d" could be slightly indicative too. One could ask, how do I tend to assess what I believe in? The answer to that question may illustrate whether the availability cascade is a factor or not.

The Availability Heuristic

Question 5 is about the availability heuristic and is relatively similar to the attentional bias as it is a mental shortcut that relies on immediate examples that come to a given person's mind when evaluating a specific topic, concept, method or decision. The availability heuristic operates on the notion that if something can be recalled, it must be important, or at least more important than alternative solutions which are not as readily recalled. Subsequently, under the availability heuristic, people tend to heavily weigh their judgments toward more recent information, making new opinions biased toward that latest news. If that news is regarding an outbreak of a virus, for example, then much of what is then discussed or decided can be justified, reasoned and argued by using the virus outbreak, purely as it is the most available content.

Answer "c" is the most obvious sign of this, although there is a slight risk with answers "a" and "b" that the heuristic may be at play. To ensure it is reduced, think of a recent major decision you made. How did you prioritize the information you used to assess your options? This approach forces reasoning, or at least creates some insight into the influential factors of our decisions.

The Mere Exposure Effect

Question 6 is about the mere-exposure effect, a psychological phenomenon by which people tend to develop a preference for things merely because they are familiar with them. In social psychology, this effect is sometimes called the familiarity principle. The effect has been demonstrated with many kinds of things, including words, paintings, pictures of faces, geometric figures, and sounds. I have noticed this a great deal in the communications world where choices in marketing campaign creation seem to be made on preferences that are simply down to the fact that those choices are seen more than others. A colour scheme, a type of haircut; a particular stance a model uses.

Answer "b" is the primary indicator with "d" in second place. This particular question requires a high degree of introspection as the tendency for the mere-exposure effect to happen can be very subtle. We may be falling prey to it without realising. Two questions that can assist in addressing this effect are as follows: Is my familiarity with what is in front of me impacting my thinking about it? If I were less familiar with it, how would my decisions be different?

The Bandwagon Effect

Question 7 is about The Bandwagon Effect. This is a phenomenon whereby the rate of uptake of beliefs, ideas, fads and trends increases the more that they have already been adopted by others. I have noticed an extraordinarily high volume of this effect happens when a competitor does something such as launch a product or make an announcement. The bandwagon effect is characterized by the probability of individual or corporate adoption increasing with respect to the proportion that has already done so. As more people come to believe in something, others also "hop on the bandwagon" regardless of the underlying evidence. The mobile phone industry is an example of an industry that seems to present these traits. I suspect this is because they have a lucrative market of consumers who are extremely keen on buying whatever the 'latest' model is, regardless of whether there are any innovative features. This, in turn, could encourage the manufacturers to de-prioritize innovation and push a wholly commercial agenda to the forefront. The mobile phone industry is just one of many examples of this, but the effect happens in all industries all of the time.

Answer "d" is the biggest signpost of this, but so is "b" to a lesser extent. As with many of these, it is often tough to have spotted it happening until we look in hindsight at the decisions that brought our current circumstances forward. In addressing the bandwagon effect, two powerful questions we could ask are: How much of our decision-making is being influenced by what another organization/person is doing? How much action would we take if they had not done anything first?

Salience Bias

Question 8 relates to Salience Bias (also known as perceptual salience) which is the cognitive bias that essentially encourages people to focus on items that are more prominent or emotionally striking and ignore those that are unremarkable, even though this difference is often irrelevant by objective standards. Salience bias is closely related to the concept of availability in behavioral economics. I personally call this the "Bright Shiny Object Trap" and it is very common across all sizes of business. I have seen decisions being made based on the attractiveness of a concept, with no other factors considered whatsoever.

Answers "c" and "d" are indicators of the salience bias being at play. Like several other biases, this is down to reasoning. Two questions that could be used to address the risk of this bias happening are: Have the relative merits been properly assessed rationally? What are the downsides of this thing, despite how attractive it is?

Groupthink

Question 9 is about a cognitive bias known as Groupthink. This is a psychological phenomenon that occurs within a group of people in which the desire for harmony or conformity in the group results in an irrational or dysfunctional decision-making outcome. At a cellular level, humans are wired for collaboration when in groups and the protection of the group becomes a priority once in it. Group members try to minimize conflict and reach a consensus decision without critical evaluation of alternative viewpoints by actively suppressing dissenting viewpoints, and by isolating themselves from outside influences.

Answers "c" and potentially "d" are indicators of this. The two primary questions to ask if we wish to avoid groupthink bias is: How much of my decision-making is based on not wishing to cause conflict? Am I sure that the main opinion of the group is valid?

Chapter 4: The Certain

"No great deed is done by falterers who ask for certainty." – George Eliot

Constituents of this grouping of characteristics are generally disposed to attempt to continue to exist in a comfort zone for as long a time as is possible. Change, for them, is frightening new territory. The hazard for people like this is the reality that change is the only thing that is predictably constant.

The following biases are particularly prevalent among members of this group:

Choice-Supportive Bias

Question 10 is all about Choice-Supportive Bias, which is sometimes known as Post-Purchase Rationalization. This is the tendency to retroactively ascribe positive attributes to an option one has selected and/or to demote the forgone options. It is a distinct cognitive bias that occurs once a decision is made. For example, if a person chooses option A instead of option B, they are likely to ignore or downplay the faults of option A while amplifying or subscribing new negative faults to option B. Conversely, they are also likely to notice and amplify the advantages of option A and not notice or de-emphasize those of option B. One example of this that I observed was Steve Russell, chief executive of Boots, who launched a health care strategy designed to differentiate the stores from competitors and grow through new health care services such as dentistry. It turned out, though, that Boots managers did not have the skills needed to succeed in health care services, and many of these markets offered little profit potential. The strategy contributed to Russell's early departure from the top job. The data he gathered about diversification created a choice-supportive bias that forced a rejection of all other data, despite that data showing clearly that the management did not have the skills. At Microsoft, Steve Ballmer also demonstrated a Choice-Supportive Bias when he forecast that the iPhone was never going to be a business phone because it does not possess any keys. Business phones had always had keys and this new challenger was therefore deemed doomed because it lacked them.

Answer "b" is the most obvious signpost of this. Regardless of your answer, there is still a useful method of ensuring you do not use the bias unconsciously. List the merits of your thoughts regarding the stimuli without using any past data or experience as justification. What are the real merits of the options in front of me - not just the ones that you prefer to be in place? It is a meaty process but worth it if you apply the effort.

Belief Bias

Question 11 is about the Belief bias. This is the tendency to judge the strength of arguments based on the *plausibility* of their conclusion rather than how strongly they support that conclusion. In certain decision-making contexts, someone with a strong belief bias can cause all manner of issues that logic, science or truth can barely address. What I have seen countless times is that a person is more likely to accept an argument that supports a conclusion that aligns with his or her values, beliefs and prior knowledge, while rejecting counter arguments to the conclusion. As the saying goes, "Never play chess with a pigeon. The pigeon just knocks all the pieces over. Then defecates all over the board. Then struts around like it won."

The obvious answer that illustrates this is "c". However, I have witnessed people with a heavy belief bias who would consider themselves as highly rational. Due to this, there are two further questions that may help determine whether the bias is at play: How much of my conclusion is being structured by a pre-existing decision I have made? Without that influence, would my decision or thought be the same? If those questions are answered as truthfully as possible, with a deep level of inquisition, then the answers should be insightful.

Confirmation Bias

Question 12 introduces confirmation bias, which is the tendency to search for, interpret, favor, and recall information in a way that confirms one's pre-existing beliefs or hypotheses. This, in conjunction with the argumentative theory of reasoning (question 27) and the halo effect (coming shortly), is how I explain Steve Ballmer's decision-making style. It is a type of cognitive bias and a systematic error of inductive reasoning. People display this bias when they gather or remember information selectively, or when they interpret it in a biased way. The effect is stronger for desired outcomes, emotionally charged issues, and for deeply entrenched-beliefs. Confirmation bias is extraordinarily common and often includes an emotional mechanism within it. Take the case of Wang Laboratories, the top company in the word-processing industry in the early 1980s. Recognizing that his company's future was threatened by the rise of the personal computer, founder An Wang built a machine to compete in this sector. Unfortunately, he chose to create a proprietary operating system despite the fact that the IBM personal computer was clearly becoming the dominant standard in the industry. This blunder, which contributed to Wang's demise a few years later, was heavily influenced by An Wang's dislike of IBM. He believed he had been cheated by IBM over a new technology he had invented early in his career. These feelings made him reject a software platform linked to an IBM product even though the platform was provided by a third party, Microsoft.

Answer "a" is the most obvious indicator, but answer "d" also suggests it (with a level of willingness to address it too). The two most powerful questions that can be applied here are: What is my decision-making criteria? Am I thinking this thing because I prefer to or is it because I have rationally considered the other options?

Illusory Correlation

Question 13 is about Illusory Correlation. In psychology, illusory correlation is the phenomenon of perceiving a relationship between variables (typically those variables are people, events, or behaviours) even when no such relationship exists. It is similar to the Gambler's Fallacy that we will explain in the answers to question 22. However, illusory correlation is less about forming an opinion based on a vague, observed pattern that serves a purpose and more about creating an entirely fictitious set of assumptions without there being any pattern in the first place. Such a false association may be formed because rare or novel occurrences are more salient and therefore tend to capture one's attention. If a business leader realizes that the most highly performing sales staff were all hired on Wednesdays, he or she may well make an illusory correlation between that specific day of the week and sales performance.

Answer "c" and potentially "d" are the two main signposts. A good question to ask, when seeking to avoid this bias, is: How likely is this data to actually be random? What supports it being correlated or not correlated? It is only in this inquisition that we can more accurately work out whether information is linked.

Escalation of Commitment

Question 14 relates to Escalation Of Commitment. This is a human behavior pattern where an individual or group faces increasingly negative outcomes from a decision or action, but nevertheless continues the behavior instead of altering course. It can be observed when an executive maintains behaviors that are irrational but seems to align with previous decisions and actions. The commitment escalates over time as more investment into the activity has been made. This is similar to the choice supportive bias, but with an additional "increasing investment" element. There is also a variation known as the "Sunk Cost Trap" which is also based on the tendency for people to irrationally follow through on an activity that is not meeting their expectations. This is because of the time and/or money they have already invested.

Answers "b" and "d" are the biggest signs of escalation of commitment. The two most powerful questions I have found to ask are: "What parts of our decision-making is based on factors leading up to this moment?" And: "If we were to eliminate the most recent events/decisions, would we be making the same decisions?"

Status Quo Bias

Question 15 is about Status quo bias. Unsurprisingly, the status quo bias is a preference for the current state of affairs. The current baseline (or status quo) is taken as a reference point, and any change from that baseline is perceived as a loss. I have observed this frequently affecting human decision-making in all sizes of enterprise. One could suspect it to be an "old-school" issue, but it is just as common in tiny start-ups as it is in giant blue-chip organizations. People mainly want to feel comfortable and stable.

Answer "a" is obviously the biggest signpost of this bias. The ways I have addressed this with people is to firstly ask: How can we assess the risk of inaction caused by us choosing not to change things? Then, it is often valuable to develop two or more scenarios where elements of stability or comfort have been adjusted but still are able to drive growth opportunities.

The Ostrich Effect

Question 16 is about the Ostrich Effect. This is where truth is hidden to avoid information that may be seen as negative. What I have observed is that junior staff miss out about 20 per cent of the truth in their reporting upwards, middle management then remove another 40 per cent, senior management get rid of about 20 per cent and the board of directors have a fraction of the picture presented to them. The reason for this effect is a combination of fear and greed: fear of getting fired or reprimanded and greed for getting promoted or rewarded.

Answers "d" and "c" indicate there may be a risk of the ostrich effect happening and it could be useful to consider: what are the longer term impacts of shielding the truth from others? What levels of authenticity do I value in myself? How would I feel if the full picture was not shown to me?

Not Invented Here

Question 17 is about a concept called Not Invented Here. This is a stance adopted by people and organizations that avoid using or buying already existing products, research, or knowledge because of their external origins and costs. I have observed that it is extremely common to hold a strong bias against ideas from the outside. A senior executive at a large telecommunication company once told me that "under no circumstances will we use technology we do not develop in-house". I have found it exceptionally difficult to assist people in overcoming this bias through the years, despite reams of evidence relating to the power of collaboration.

Answers "a" and "c" are the biggest signposts of this bias potentially being at play. One useful method to try in combatting the bias is to ask this type of question: If it were to be proven that an externally invented idea would be highly beneficial to you and/or your organization, how would you adjust your thinking to enable that external idea to be used? This essentially forces a scenario to happen with the words "highly beneficial" included, to hopefully attract a willingness to experiment with the scenario.

Chapter 5: The Gambler

"There is no fool like a careless gambler who starts taking victory for granted." – Hunter S Thompson

Individuals displaying the characteristics of this category of person are likely to weigh up chances and place "bets," literally or figuratively, on potential outcomes with different probabilities of occurring. That exposes them to making decisions with a low level of rationality. Members of this group are particularly subject to the following biases:

Hyperbolic Discounting

Question 18 is about Hyperbolic Discounting. In economics, hyperbolic discounting is a time-inconsistent model of delay discounting. It is one of the cornerstones of behavioural economics. In its simplest form this refers to the tendency for people to increasingly choose a smaller-sooner reward over a larger-later reward as the delay occurs sooner rather than later in time. Humans are said to discount the value of the later reward, by a factor that increases with the length of the delay. In business, this often comes into play in the minds of leaders and budget-owners who are measured and rewarded on relatively short-term goals, such as quarterly reports. With this in place, we rarely see a delayed reward as more valuable even if it is unarguably of enhanced value.

Answers "a" and "c" are the most obvious pointers towards hyperbolic discounting being a factor in our thoughts. Remember, this is not necessarily a "bad" thing. There are no wrong answers. However, it is useful to understand where our tendencies are, especially as advertisers and marketers often use our tendencies to persuade us. To address this bias, perhaps ask yourself these questions: What is my choice of smaller-sooner or larger-later based upon? Could I calculate the chances of the longer-term outcome more accurately?

The Neglect of Probability

Question 19 is about the Neglect of Probability Bias which is the tendency to disregard probability when making a decision under uncertainty. Small risks are typically either neglected entirely or hugely overrated. The continuum between the extremes is ignored. This is a really popular way in which people regularly violate the normative rules for decision-making. Normative theory refers to identifying the best decision to take, assuming an ideal decision maker who is fully informed, able to compute with perfect accuracy, and fully rational.

Being unaware of the risks inherent with neglect of probability, could prove to be problematic in decision-making. Due to this, answer "d" and possibly "b" are the ones to watch out for. The key point is about reasoning. Questions to ask are: How rational have I been in terms of considering other probabilities? What am I potentially missing?

Normalcy Bias

Question 20 introduces the Normalcy Bias. This is a belief people hold when considering the possibility of a disaster. It causes people to underestimate both the likelihood of a disaster and its possible effects, because people believe that things will always function the way things normally have functioned. This may result in situations where people fail to adequately prepare themselves for disasters, and on a larger scale, the failure of governments to include the populace in its disaster preparations. In 2013, Esther Inglis-Arkell wrote an article in Gizmodo that amazingly suggested that around 70 per cent of people reportedly display normalcy bias in disasters. I have seen this repeatedly in business scenario planning sessions where executives are able to imagine business disasters but seemingly unable to imagine what their regular day-to-day would look like in the imaginary context.

Answers "b" and "d" could be an issue in thought processes, mainly because they could indicate a tendency toward a normalcy bias, whether intentional or not. To address this, you could create a scenario where what you think is unlikely to happen, actually happens. Then, assess as rationally as possible, using whatever data points are available, the probability of that outcome happening.

Optimism Bias

Question 21 is about Optimism Bias which is where someone believes that they are less likely to experience a negative event. It is also known as unrealistic optimism or comparative optimism. Optimism bias is common and transcends gender, ethnicity, nationality and age. The Optimism Bias has even been reported in non-human animals such as rats and birds. Four factors exist that cause a person to be biased in this way: their desired end state, their cognitive mechanisms, the information they have about themselves versus others, and overall mood. The Optimism Bias is seen in a number of situations. For example: people believing that they are less at risk of being a crime victim, smokers believing that they are less likely to contract lung cancer than other smokers, first-time bungee jumpers believing that they are less at risk of an injury than other jumpers, or traders who think they are less exposed to losses in the markets. In my experience, this bias impacts executives in all sizes of business. For example, despite The Startup Genome project finding that 90 per cent of all startups fail, I have yet to meet more than a handful of entrepreneurs who can even conceptualize the chances of failing. In fact, I have heard multitudes of reasons why theirs will not (but many others will).

Answers "a" and "c" are the two main signposts. Remember, there are no right answers in this, and optimism is not a bad thing! Nonetheless, we could do worse than to ask: What data am I using to base my optimism upon? Are there any more rational ways of assessing probable outcomes than using the data points I have access to?

The Gambler's Fallacy

Question 22 relates to the Gambler's Fallacy, also known as the Monte Carlo Fallacy or the Fallacy of the Maturity of Chances, which is the mistaken belief that, if something happens more frequently than normal during a given period, it will happen less frequently in the future (or vice versa). This is incredibly common in all types of businesses but also in everyday life. For example, one of the challenges that insurance companies have is selling to people who have never needed to use insurance. In business, if a senior executive quits their job after being there for a few months, many other stakeholders could mistakenly feel that the next hire is more or less likely to quit after a similar period…with no evidence either way.

Answer "b" and potentially "a" are signposts of this fallacy. It is all about what information is being used to base assumptions upon. This is "correlation data". In terms of that, two potential questions could be: What correlation data am I using to form my opinion on? Is it valid or is it simply a hunch?

Chapter 6: The Inward

"I go into solitude so as not to drink out of everybody's cistern. When I am among the many, I live as the many do, and I do not think I really think. After a time, it always seems as if they want to banish my self from myself and rob me of my soul." – Friedrich Nietzsche

Folk falling into this segment have an inclination to be relatively introspective and focused on an agenda driven from within themselves. That brings with it a danger of relying too heavily on oneself and not benefiting from stimulus provided by others, which can lead to not always generating the best possible decisions. Members of this group are particularly subject to the following biases:

The False Consensus Effect

Question 23 relates to the False-Consensus Effect. This is where people tend to overestimate the extent to which their opinions, beliefs, preferences, values, and habits are normal and typical of those of others (I.E. that others also think the same way that they do). This cognitive bias tends to lead to the perception of a consensus that does not exist, a "false consensus". I see this on a daily basis. One of the ways that I have been able to qualify if the bias is in play is to consistently seek to validate the consensus. I ask questions like: "When you say: 'Everyone thinks that', how many people did you discuss this with?" or: "It would be great to get those opinions in writing at some point, just so we can see what patterns emerge." Naturally one would not want to ask these probing questions in an aggressive or an intentionally annoying manner, but it is a very useful practice to ask, otherwise we ourselves will fall victim to the same bias.

Answer "a" is the main indicator of this effect. Sometimes we do not know we are presenting this bias as it is a fairly silent thought process. The three primary questions to ask are: How have I quantified the consensus? How many people have I asked and referenced? How valid are these samples?

The Self-Serving Bias

Question 24 is about the Self-Serving Bias. This is the tendency to perceive oneself in an overly favourable manner, or when the need to maintain and enhance self-esteem distorts the way we think. It can be observed when people put success down to their own talents and activities but think that failure is based on external factors. When individuals reject the validity of negative feedback, focus on their strengths and achievements but overlook their faults and failures, or take more responsibility for their group's work than they give to other members, they are protecting their ego from threat and injury. I have always found this a fascinating bias, especially in contrast to the evidence relating to whose "fault" business failure actually is. According to the Association of Insolvency and Restructuring Advisors, when businesses fail, 52 per cent of the time it is down to internal triggers, circumstances that have nothing to do with anything outside the business. 15 per cent is down to external triggers and 24 per cent is both. 8 per cent of the time there are external factors beyond the control of the business and 1 per cent of the time it is bad luck. Put bluntly, 91 per cent of the time business fail it is down to how people in the company have seen, understood, processed and decided.

Success and failure are all about how we think.

Answers "a" and "b" are equally prime indicators of this bias. Perhaps the most powerful way of addressing it is to ask: What methods have I put in place that force me to consider less than positive feedback in a rational way? Or alternatively: How can I assess the findings in a non-emotive way that provides insight and learning?

The Pseudocertainty Effect

Question 25 is about the Pseudocertainty Effect. This is the tendency for people to perceive an outcome as certain while it is actually uncertain. It can be observed in multi-stage decision-making, in which evaluation of the certainty of the outcome in a previous stage of decisions is disregarded when selecting an option in subsequent stages. There can be a common arrogance across executives. I must say I have noticed it especially in male-dominated cultures, where this effect seems to be the common parlance. Doubt or even sensitivity seems akin to humility when it comes to attractiveness amongst like-minded egos.

Answers "b" and "c" are signposts of this effect being more likely than not. This does not mean that we should question everything, but to ensure that our certainty is valid, it may be useful to consider the following scenario: If someone outside our decision-making team was to assess our level of certainty, how similar would their assessment be to ours? If it would vary, why would that be the case? Are we over-assessing the certainty here?

The Halo Effect

Question 26 relates to The Halo Effect which is when our overall impression of a person influences how we feel and think about his or her character. Essentially, your overall impression of a person ("He is nice!") impacts your evaluations of that person's specific traits ("He is also smart!"). I have noticed that confirmation bias can make the halo effect even more powerful. Once someone has formed a positive opinion of a person (or product), any further interaction that is also positive, reinforces the positive opinion, whereas negative interactions are often cast to one side. The halo effect is why brands seek celebrity endorsements and how physically attractive people sometimes get hired at job interviews more frequently. It also partly helps explain the growth of Apple.

The company perfected the iPhone into something that would change the mobile phone industry by obsessively building it into everything that anyone ever wanted a mobile phone to do. That gave the company a following that flocked to their other innovations, such as the iPad tablet and the iWatch, thinking that they would be equally world-changing.

The reverse halo effect (sometimes called the "devil horns" effect) is also true in that a negative characteristic will make a person or product seem overall less attractive. Similarly, to the negativity bias, this cognitive bias can make negative first impressions have a much stronger impact.

Answer "a" is the biggest indicator of this bias, but "c" is not far behind. The halo effect is so popular it is fairly likely to have happened at some point in most of our lives. The three questions to address this are: What attributes am I linking together between the original piece of information and my related assumptions? Are they really linked or imagined? How can I justify any links that I have observed?

The Argumentative Theory Of Reasoning

Question 27 is about The Argumentative Theory Of Reasoning. This theory suggests that people argue for status. It has nothing to do with being right and everything to do with winning the argument. We argue to see who will get the best mates or have the highest status in the herd. Unlike the belief, which goes back to Descartes, that we argue to critically examine a position, the Argumentative Theory of Reasoning suggests that we argue for position or status. One proponent of this bias in my view is Steve Ballmer, the former Microsoft chief executive who reduced the company's stock price during his tenure by 40 per cent, partly by exhibiting it. In my opinion, Ballmer's decisions exhibited two other thought challenges: Confirmation Bias and Choice-Supportive Bias (see question 10).

Answer "a" and potentially "d" are signposts of this bias. A key method in addressing it is to analyse what it is you would like to achieve and why you find that so important? Who else will benefit from it and who would be disadvantaged by you achieving it? This analysis re-directs the focus from argumentation towards the importance of objectives.

The Observer-Expectancy Effect

Question 28 relates to the Observer-Expectancy Effect (also called the experimenter-expectancy effect, expectancy bias, observer effect, or experimenter effect). This is a form of reactivity in which a researcher's cognitive bias causes them to subconsciously influence the participants of an experiment. This is a type of confirmation bias which can lead to the experimenter interpreting results incorrectly because of the tendency to look for information that conforms to their hypothesis and overlook information that argues against it. I have observed this bias also including conscious influence and the mechanics of this range from the blatant to the subtle, including:

• Bad sampling – often seen where a very small segment of people is asked a question and the resulting percentages are scaled across a much larger population.

• Predictive questions – a modern day media classic is "would you like adverts on your mobile device?" This is predominantly asked when the required result is a resounding "no". If you want the answer to include more 'yes' responses, you would remove the word advertising and switch it for "useful content that would make your life better?" This leads to a major skew towards the positive. Either way, the questions have predictable answers.

• Misleading selections – commonly where a snapshot of real data is used which intentionally misses out preceding periods which would harm the impact – for instance, if you wanted to show an upturn in advertising spend, but only three months in a year had an increase, you would not show the downturn that happened before, only the growing months (which may well be making up a fraction of the previous loss).

- Self-adjusted rankings – the editorial right to remove any justification of ranking. In whatever industry you are in, you may have seen companies who claim to be the "World's Number 1". Surely there can only be one, right? But, from closer inspection, you find that the information not included is the part that defines exactly what ranking conditions they include. Is it in terms of revenue, profit, employee numbers or experience of the chief executive? We are only shown the juicy bits and the terms and conditions are nowhere to be seen.

- Limiting qualifiers – one of my favourites and similar to self-adjusted rankings. This is where you word a statistic in a way that the result is essentially fixed. For instance: "The brown bear is the largest land predator in the world". The word "predator" rules out elephants which are bigger but are not predators, while the word 'land' rules out various whales which are predators but do not live on land. The statement is built for the brown bear to dominate.

- Percentage accentuation – exceptionally common. Take a company making a bunch of people redundant. If the company has 100 staff and gets rid of 20, in the interests of making the statistic sexier, it would be "Company lays off 20 per cent of entire workforce!" because 20 people does not sound anywhere near as dramatic as 20 per cent. However, in a company of 1 million, the 20 per cent is still quite sexy but nothing sounds as big as "Company lays off 200,000 people!" The liberal insertion of exclamation marks is my own, of course.

Answer "d" is the most obvious signpost here, although "c" could also be displaying a risk of observer expectancy. The key is to be conscious of the potential influence we may be having, so questions such as these may help: What thoughts, feelings or actions am I processing that could influence the participants or the results of this activity? How can I limit the influence effectively?

The Bias Blind Spot

Question 29 relates to the Bias Blind Spot which is the cognitive bias of recognizing the impact of biases on the judgment of others, while failing to see the impact of biases on one's own judgment. Many leaders that I have met believe that they are the least biased people in their organization. That, in itself, is most certainly a bias blind spot!

Answers "a" and "b" are the strongest indicators of this bias. Assuming we are aware of other people's biases, the main question should be: Regardless of other people's biases, what personal biases am I potentially not paying attention to? That is the point of this entire framework of course!

Superpowered By Thought

The range of heuristics and biases that I have just presented are fuelled often by business processes that are simply not structured to enable optimal thought but often have an exclusive objective of profit or sales. The way that hierarchical promotion tends to work is more of a political framework rather than a meritocracy; based on a quality of thinking that could set the company on a bigger growth curve. Even the way that offices are designed, or furniture chosen, has an impact on how we think, but many companies under prioritize these aspects too.

As today is the slowest pace of change we'll ever experience, to enable Advanced Thought requires us to work on our thought muscle as much as any other. In general, the issues of thought are common to *untrained thought*. They are the result of a lack of critical thinking and a lack of effort to enable optimal thought performance. Every one of these heuristics and biases are due to a weakness or laziness in our thinking which enable a reliance on our heuristics and biases to essentially "step in" and intervene. The heuristics and biases are *shortcuts* that, without realizing, do not actually provide an optimal outcome or a more efficient result. Instead, they return sub-optimal decisions which determine our fate. Add to that the constant winds of change, we are at risk of trying to build a wall rather than a windmill, or just being blown away.

What is needed is for thought to be viewed as a *muscle* in its own right and then for us to methodologically exercise our muscle properties on a regular basis. The next section will build such a methodology to help us train our brains so that our bodies and businesses are capable of meeting outrageous goals.

Section Two: Understanding and Training our Thought Muscle

Chapter 7: Five Qualities of the Thought Muscle

"Nothing stops the man who desires to achieve. Every obstacle is simply a course to develop his achievement muscle. It's a strengthening of his powers of accomplishment." – Thomas Carlyle

The standard view of muscles holds true in terms of the need for nourishment and exercise. However, much of our traditional muscle strength (in our arms and legs for example) comes from our mind. According to a study published in the Journal of Neurophysiology, a large degree of muscle strength is derived from the way that the human brain operates, rather than from the consistency of the muscles themselves. In <u>research carried out at the Musculoskeletal and Neurological Institute of Ohio University</u>, 29 volunteers had their non-dominant arms placed in casts spanning the length from their elbow to their fingers for four weeks. A separate collection of 15 individuals carried on as normal, without such casts. 14 of the 29 in the first group were asked to perform mental-imagery exercises for five out of the seven days in every week, imagining themselves alternately flexing and resting their immobilized wrists for five-second intervals. After the end of the experiment, following four weeks, members of both groups reported having lost strength in their arms. However, the group that had imagined themselves doing the arm exercises had shed significantly less, measuring an average of 25 per cent weaker than at the start of the study, compared to 45 per cent for the group that had not taken part in the mental imagery activities. It can be concluded from the study that it appears that muscular nourishment and exercise is primarily needed for our brain.

So, if we are to consider thought as a muscle, first we need to understand what a "normal" muscle is, in other words - the muscles that we normally class as such. Half of your body weight is muscle, and all muscle cells share four properties that differentiate them from other cells.

Excitability is the ability to respond to a stimulus. What is our normal reaction when we touch a boiling kettle? We immediately retract our hand. This is known as stimulus and the human body is programmed to respond to stimuli. The muscle tissues in our body send signals to the brain and the brain tells the body to move out – this happens within a fraction of a second. Had this taken any longer, we would have burnt our hand up until the time our brain told us to remove it. All of this is possible because of the excitability function of the muscle tissues.

Contractility is the ability of muscle cells to forcefully shorten. For instance, in order to flex (decrease the angle of a joint) your elbow you need to contract (shorten) the biceps brachii and other elbow flexor muscles in the anterior arm. Notice that in order to extend your elbow, the posterior arm extensor muscles need to contract. Thus, muscles can only pull, never push.

Extensibility is the ability of a muscle to be stretched. In order to be able to flex the elbow, the elbow extensor muscles must extend in order to allow flexion to occur. Lack of extensibility is known as spasticity.

Elasticity is the ability to recoil or bounce back to the muscle's original length after being stretched.

There are some parallels here between normal muscle cells and the properties of our thought muscle. However, I believe that these properties do not translate especially well to something that is so dynamic as thought. Let us look at each property through the lens of thought as a muscle. Although the excitability response is vital in our normal muscles, I relate more to the teachings of psychiatrist Viktor Frankl who said *"Between stimulus and response there is a space. In that space is our power to choose our response. In our response lies our growth and our freedom."* So, with thought, the excitability of our normal muscles could well be aided by the addition of a *pause* between what we experience and what we then respond with. I will return to this later in the exercises contained within the final section of this book.

In terms of contractility, one of the commonalities of sub-optimal performance as illustrated in the first section of this book, is the forceful shortening of thought. Many of the heuristics and biases are able to thrive due to the contraction of thought. They are restricting movement and, essentially, closing down the opportunity to extend. However, the opposite argument applies with thought when considering the importance of focus and persistence. In the circumstance of needing to buckle down and concentrate, components such as social media, daily news and message alerts, are counter-productive distractions. In these contexts, contractility would be useful. Again, we will return to this in the exercises that can be found later in this book.

On face value, extensibility (the ability to be extended or stretched) is perhaps the most resonant with our metaphor of thought as a muscle. As I have shown, I believe in the importance of thought being able to be stretched. However, a 2006 study by Folpp et al argued and concluded that regular stretching of muscles increased tolerance rather than extensibility. This was enhanced four years later by Weppler and Magnusson who discussed that a new sensory theory had been proposed suggesting that increases in muscle extensibility are due to a modification of sensation only, rather than actual extensibility. In the context of thought, the sensation-only of extensibility could arguably be a business poison if not coupled with *actual* extensibility. The "knowing/doing trap" is exceptionally common amongst business people who feel as if they are innovating or evolving, purely because they *think* they are - rather than actually innovating or evolving. We will return to this in the exercises found later in this book.

Elasticity in normal muscle taxonomy is all about the return to original state. In thought, though, the return to original state may be fuelling the heuristics and biases discussed in the first section. It is subjectively down to whether the original state is one of optimal performance or not. Due to the dynamic nature of thought, elasticity could be better defined as "the return to an optimal state" if indeed that state had been attained.

Muscle Properties of Thought

Late historians Will and Ariel Durant spent four decades of their lives studying, compiling, and writing the history of Western civilisation. The product of their efforts, "The Complete Story of Civilisation", went on to span several million words across more than 8,800 pages divided into 11 books. After finishing the last one, they took on an arguably more daunting task: to summarise all they had learned into 100 pages in "The Lessons of History". It is an incomplete and generalising attempt, no doubt, but it is also one of the most densely packed sources of modern wisdom available to us, provided we have a high degree of flexibility of thought that drives a perpetual curiosity to understand from the past. There are many trends and patterns to be found in history, and the Durants do a commendable job of highlighting them. The essence of their view, however, can be summarised by the following sentence:

"The only real revolution is in the enlightenment of the mind and the improvement of character, the only real emancipation is individual, and the only real revolutionists are philosophers and saints."

I love that quote. The point made, in my understanding, is one of *internal* revolution *prior* to external activities. For that to happen, we need a deep understanding of what and why we are thinking. I believe we need to understand our habit loops and inherit a disassociation between our identity and the thinking we experience.

It is critical to understand that our thoughts are constructed by the heuristics and biases that I mentioned earlier, and that they are not immovable. Equally, decisions that are made can be reversible if we design our business processes to be that way. My view is that such thoughts can be controlled, after we have become aware of them and understood their implications by directly confronting head-on the internal processes and biases that led to their development. If we can be aware that our thoughts are manufactured constructs and if we can understand what the thoughts are and why we are thinking like we do; we can then deconstruct our patterns effectively.

To such an extent, one could draw a parallel between the traditional muscles of the human body and thought being a muscle in and of itself. In contrast to the traditional properties of normal muscles which are mechanical, I consider our metaphorical muscular properties of thought to be aesthetic by nature. Aesthetics is the branch of philosophy concerned with the nature and appreciation of art, beauty and good taste. It has also been defined as "critical reflection on art, culture and nature". The word "aesthetics" derives from the Greek "aisthetikos", meaning "of sense perception". Along with ethics, aesthetics is part of axiology (the study of values and value judgements). The properties I will outline in this section are not to be confused with muscular fitness aesthetics however, where the term means the pleasant, positive or artful appearance of a person or a thing. Here, I am not concerned with how things look but how thought is functionally constructed.

- **A Clarity of Response**

Clarity of thought not only includes the clear definition of what we are thinking, but also includes the understanding and ability to not think, to not reflexively see thinking as the only way to experience the world. Clarity of thought is one's ability to gather and differentiate all incoming stimuli into a clear definition to position the mind with resolve.

On the road to clarity, confusion starts by blocking our access to what is meaningful and leads us to indecisiveness. We are misunderstood by everyone including ourselves and eventually we lose our authenticity. Clarity in thoughts is very important.

Brendon Burchard, the author of High Performance Habits: How Extraordinary People Become That Way, says Oprah Winfrey starts every meeting the same way: She says:

"What is our intention for this meeting? What is important? What matters?"

Why does she start a meeting that way? High performers like Oprah constantly seek clarity. They work hard to sift out distractions, so they do not just focus, but *continually* re-focus, on what is important. That is because clarity is not something you get. Clarity is something you have to *seek* - you only find clarity and focus when you actively search for it.

In the Forbes article from 2015 entitled "In Business, Clarity Comes First", the author makes a very clear point about the theme:

"Here is the secret about clarity: it takes work to achieve. There is no magic formula for ensuring that people are aligned and share a common understanding of the mission or task at hand. The only way to succeed is for all team members, regardless of rank or position, to make sure that clarity comes first in all interactions."

The piece goes on to state that, although bringing about clarity is the responsibility of the leader of an organization, success in achieving that objective remains very much a team effort. If something is not clear, staff need to say so and make an effort to resolve the difficulty. In this way, clarity with corporates becomes a "two-way street," with all participants required to take part on an equal basis.

"The most important thing is to make the effort," it continues. *"If you manage to foster a culture of clarity inside of your organization, you will see fewer problems, better execution, and happier, more productive teams."*

I relate to this view and I even summarized it in a 2019 article for CEO Today magazine on what leaders could learn from Brexit:

- Leaders need to ensure extreme clarity of a vision that is productive. This is an on-going activity and can be tested by checking with stakeholders to understand what their version of your vision is and whether it is seen as productive moving forward.

- Leaders need to be brave in taking positive actions. They must reduce or remove activities that do not assist or enable the vision to manifest. These are not welcome.

- Leaders need to side-line any selfish ambition that does not enable the vision to come to life. If, however, the vision and actions will enable personal ambition to be realized, that is positive. Remember, this is not promoting altruism. It is promoting an alignment of the components to ensure the opportunity is captured.

These operate in series. They stem from clarity. The ability to remove noise and focus on the signal is something I have spoken about on many stages around the world and is something that I believe will become more salient as a focus in a world of increasing connectivity. Noise is the enemy of signal and therefore the nemesis of clarity. To counteract noise, I will present exercises to enable us to "de-noise" in the final section of this book. In my opinion, clarity is the starting point that enables all other properties to strongly perform.

- **The Strength to Persist**

The second thought property I would like to propose is strength. I see strength in this metaphorical context as being how thoughts construct new versions of what is (or was) considered to be an obstacle. This activity of reframing obstacles is, in my opinion, the highest capability of thought strength. It has certainly been of personal importance in my life.

Those of you who have read *Powered by Change* may remember the section on my background. My upbringing was peppered with an array of seemingly negative circumstances. From being given up at birth to being violently bullied and abused through my school years of 5 to 16 (bookmarked with being stabbed at both ages), my early days were challenging. As I progressed into adulthood, I was relatively successful in business until I was viciously ripped-off by my close friend and business partner. Starting from zero again, but this time with a young family in tow, I then re-built my career over ten years only to be yet again taken to the cleaners by a different close friend and business partner. At the time of writing this, I am back restructuring many professional contexts. But this time I am armed with the lessons that I did not listen nor learn from last time.

From casual observation it would seem that my life has been full of obstacles. Painful hurdles in a game that seemed to be rigged against me. However, from the first stabbing to the most recent experience, I have worked hard at viewing these circumstances as opportunities to grow rather than evidence that I am going to always lose. This requires a strength of thought: the strength to not give up, not stand down and not roll-over. These activities are not possible without thought as they require a decision to be made at each juncture. Personally, I decided that I could rise above the abuse. I am not suggesting that this was easy and "hey, it is simple to just shrug things off" – instead I believe that we have a choice in how we respond. That choice is a strength and if we tap into it, we can choose to respond in ways to become a more fulfilled upgrade of who we were yesterday.

One of the reasons that I have achieved all my coin flip objectives is that I was able to re-frame what was "impossible", "improbable" or "not something I am able to achieve" into "possible", "likely" and "completed". This requires strength of thought but also the ability for thought to impact a positive set of behaviours.

There is a definite mindset that is important here, but it is not just about positive thinking. In order to remain focused on the goal in a way that is likely to lead to it being achieved, individuals and organizations need to develop resolve and persistence. I would go as far to suggest that these qualities need to be embedded deep in our thoughts and the actions that those thoughts influence and direct.

If we return to the example of Nike's corporate purpose, the declarations therein only have any effect if there is a corporate will to make sure that they resonate authentically in everything that the company does. The process to achieve this usually relies on chains of responsibility, direct reporting lines and clear accountability - but strength of thought goes even further. Without inflicting the Groupthink (that I described earlier) on the organization, everybody within it needs to buy into its goals and ambitions.

- **A Recognition of the Likely Impact of Actions**

The third property is impact. I mean this in the context of behavioural benefit or how our thoughts enable a new or continued beneficial behaviour. Thoughts that would score less on impact would be thoughts that drive a low or non-existent impact from whatever resultant behaviour comes next. For instance, in the status quo bias where there is a preference for the current state of affairs and any change from that baseline is perceived as a loss, the impact of that thought is that our behaviour repeats the same patterns as it always has done. We do not evolve, we do not learn, and we do not improve.

The alternative is when thought results in a great benefit such as in Wal-Mart where Sam Walton's decision to hold Saturday morning, all-employee meetings led to a culture of rapid information and decision-making, which in turn created one of the biggest companies in the world. Or in Apple when the board's decision to bring back Steve Jobs, after firing him a decade earlier, led to amazing product innovation and to the creation of one of the most valuable companies in the world. Or in Ford where Henry Ford's decision to double the wages of his workers enabled him to attract the talent he needed and helped ensure a class of worker who could afford the very products they were building.

In the book "Tough Calls From The Corner Office" by Harlan Steinbaum, the author uses 40 examples of the most positively impactful decisions and how the CEOs made them. The Wharton interview with the author is fascinating in that it shows a similarity throughout every example. That similarity is in how little the negative cognitive biases were evidently at play. We may never know exactly what was going through their heads at the time, but the outcomes strongly suggest that these are not "standard" decisions that business people make. As Steinbaum says at the end of the Wharton interview, *"the best way to make a defining-moment decision is to study all the facts, learn everything you can about the circumstances you are in, the pros and cons, the cost-benefit analysis, and then make your decision. It has really got to be thought out."*

The leaders all show an elevated perspective to the challenge at hand. These decisions were made by people who, in my opinion, overcame their biases by overlaying curiosity, bravery, and a clearly defined purpose. The impact of this is enhanced even further with the ability to expand and contract in a flexible manner.

- ### A Flexibility of Thought

Flexibility is the quality of bending easily without breaking, the ability to be easily modified and the willingness to change or compromise. Thoughts can flex horizontally across a range of contexts and subjects and vertically, elevating or deepening in a particular area. They can do both flexes at once, enabling a highly elevated perspective across a vast area of themes. In *Powered by Change,* I argue that our ability to innovate is directly proportional to our ability to elevate. The way I quantify flexibility as a property of thought is to observe how thoughts are increased through perpetual curiosity and willingness to increase understanding. Flexibility allows us to develop imaginative contexts to be considered as if real, thus preparing us for sub-optimal circumstances or widening our opportunities to maximise growth. I do not see flexibility as just being about "thinking differently". Instead, I see it as being highly elastic in the ways that thoughts are conceived and processed.

One of my favourite examples of flexibility is from George Lucas. As recounted in the article on the StartUpMindset website in 2017, before Lucas alighted upon the concept of a "western set in space," that he initially entitled "The Star Wars" in 1971, he was still making his way as a Hollywood film director with just two full-length movie credits - THX 1138 and American Graffiti. American Graffiti's box office achievements earned Lucas a chance to produce and direct Star Wars and provided him with an opportunity to make $500,000 on the project – more than three times the $150,000 he had realized from his previous film. It was actually an offer that his bosses at 20th Century Fox thought they would never have to pay out on, since they did not fully comprehend the concept behind the movie and thought it unlikely to earn them serious money.

Lucas responded by offering instead to peg his salary at $150,000, as long as he could retain all merchandizing rights and the rights to any sequels.

The agreement of the Fox directors to his proposal needs to be understood in the context of the concept of multiple films under a single banner not really taking off until the 1970s. Fox executives were also only scarred by their experience of having made heavy losses from the merchandizing connected to the Doctor Dolittle concept in the 1960s. However, history does not look kindly upon their decision, with Star Wars going on to gross a new record for the film industry, with receipts of more than $27 billion from ticket sales and the merchandizing of videos, toys, books, and other licensed products. Lucas benefited hugely, owning 100 per cent of the Star Wars franchise until he sold the company to Disney for $4 billion in 2012. He is now said to be worth more than $5 billion. Astonishingly, Lucas has only directed six feature films in his entire career, and four of them were Star Wars movies. His success is a supreme example of flexibility of thought. Lucas did not succeed here because he was a better negotiator or a more skilled salesman. What enabled his triumph was the ability of his mind to not only come up with a highly-creative science fiction concept but also a completely new way of monetizing the conventional US movie business.

In my view, every good example of thinking shows a high degree of flexibility in thought. You do not have to be a large, wealthy company to be flexible, nor do you need to be a household brand name. Flexibility, as demonstrated in the Star Wars example, involves the curiosity to explore and develop new business as well as creative concepts, the bravery to not be dissuaded from a vision by past failures and a clearly defined individual or corporate purpose. Curiosity is defined here as constantly searching for new ways of experiencing and learning. Bravery means constantly taking chances to experiment even in lesser-known areas of business, while purpose signifies the clarification of exactly what business you are truly in. Again, this was detailed in *Powered by Change* in the first of the four "Windmill blades".

The volume of thought drives us to be perpetually curious and willing to increase our understanding. This combination is what has fuelled the coin flips but is also the reason I often take up new academic studies, most recently an intensive course in neuro-economics via the Higher School of Economics at the National Research University, studying under Vasily Klucharev, Professor and Head of the Department of Psychology. This is not the last course that I take and to be honest, I feel as if I am only scratching the surface of what can be newly understood. Actually, that neuro-economics course dismantled a great deal of what I thought I knew about how we operate and has propelled me back to questioning everything I thought I knew before. To be honest, the course is one of the reasons this book exists. Flexibility requires alignment so that thoughts are directed and positioned in the most resonant way with ourselves and others.

- **True Alignment with Personal or Corporate Values**

The quality of our thoughts can also be measured by how aligned they are to our personal and corporate values. This becomes highly significant if we accept that what and how we think actually determines every outcome that we experience. This is easier to demonstrate among individuals than in organizations, due to the increased complexity that corporates generate as they grow, adding different areas of operation and importing other cultures through acquisitions or joint ventures. Yet, the strength of leadership shown by entrepreneurs such as Sir Richard Branson, Sir James Dyson, Bill Gates, Steve Jobs and other modern business icons proves that it can be translated across to the corporate arena. It is commonly said that the stronger the link between corporate values and the personal values of the leadership, the greater the chance the organization has of sustainable success…but of course it is wider than simply leadership. The truth is that the stronger the link is between corporate and personal values within our staff, team, stakeholders, partners, customers, clients and the public in general, the greater the chance of market acceptance, adoption and success.

One of the most beneficial leadership traits that I have observed is for a leader to set an extremely clear ambition for the group, justified by a set of clear values which are communicated in a way that people understand. This is followed by making decisions that are evidently aligned to the underlying values.

A great example of such alignment is WD-40, the California-based manufacturer of household and multi-use products, including its signature brand WD-40, but also 3-In-1 Oil, Lava, Spot Shot, X-14, Carpet Fresh, GT85, 1001, Solvol, 2000 Flushes and No Vac. At the time of writing, it markets products in more than 176 countries. Garry Ridge, the chief executive who calls himself the "chief" of the WD-40 "tribe," is a brilliant example of thought alignment. He claims that creating lasting memories in his staff's minds is one of the keys to having built success during his several decades as the leader. I reckon his creation of a trust-based and respect-based culture is also majorly important. He says *"Leadership is about learning and teaching. Why waste getting old if you can not get wise? We have no mistakes here; we have learning moments"*.

In his insightful interview with Forbes he explains why he believes the annual performance review process is broken, instead placing coaching, development, and feedback as an everyday conversation between leader and direct report, a theme often noted in his 2009 book, co-authored with Ken Blanchard, 'Helping People Win at Work: A Business Philosophy Called "Do not Mark My Paper, Help Me Get an A."'

At WD-40, employee engagement numbers are in excess of 90 per cent and shareholder value has grown consistently over the past 14 years. Ridge describes how a focus on the servant leadership principles of values, learning, teaching, growth, and community can lead to enhanced performance by helping people step into the best version of themselves. This is thought muscle alignment exemplified.

These aesthetic yet functional properties of thought comprise what I believe to be an optimal state that would enable us to make better decisions. This state is what I class as using Advanced Thought, and when maximised, these properties address the reliance on the heuristics and biases we are prone to.

If you search online for ways to get physically fit you will find a mountain of information, ranging from gym membership adverts to tips and tricks to "get better abs" or "improve muscle tone". Performing an online search for "train your thoughts" provides a smaller cross-section of results, in amongst a plethora of brain training apps. Interestingly, the results tend to be based on thinking positively or becoming happy. Perhaps the Roman Emperor, Marcus Aurelius, had the right idea when he said: *"The happiness of your life depends upon the quality of your thoughts."* The main advice seems to include:

- Focus on what makes you happy
- Turn negatives into positives
- Look after your health
- Sleep better
- Let go
- Do not judge
- Stay calm
- Think differently

These are good pointers and I imagine they must be worth something as they are repeated in multiple ways by numerous experts. Personally, I feel that more is required in terms of specific exercises that work the different properties of our thought muscle. As with our traditional muscles, ignoring one property runs a risk of it decaying and the overall body being less capable as a result. Due to our tendency to live in a repeat cycle, we tend to focus on the things that we feel comfortable about. In the gym, this often manifests as a sense of comfort doing certain exercises that we can "do well". This is also particularly the case at a corporate level and can lead to complacency and failure to adapt to new realities that require different skill-sets, as the failures of video rental chain Blockbuster and film-maker Eastman Kodak demonstrate.

In the following chapters, my aim is to give a more thorough exposition of each quality of thought, complete with examples of how it presents itself among our leading companies and executives. Each of our five qualities of thought is also given a section for your own workout, with an array of exercises that will enable you to truly step into your Advanced Thought.

Chapter 8: Mind Flip 1: Developing a Clarity of Response

"We can learn the art of fierce compassion, redefining strength, deconstructing isolation and renewing a sense of community, practicing letting go of rigid us-versus-them thinking, while cultivating power and clarity in response to difficult situations." – Sharon Salzberg

Gaining clarity is the most effective way to stop our thoughts from becoming problematic, sub-optimal or destructive.

The health and wellness industry is worth nearly $5 trillion a year globally. The gyms industry is growing by a double-digit percentage, with new outlets even being opened within workplaces so that employees do not have far to move during their lunch breaks. Smoothie and juice bars are also opening apace and there is growing demand for "healthier" food products such as pulses and quinoa and alternative drinks including hemp and oat milk. Human beings are spending increasing amounts of money trying to "fix" themselves or become healthier and most developed economies now teach our children from a very young age that regular exercise and nutrient-dense foods are the recipe for a long and healthy life.

Despite all this laudable emphasis on health and well-being, however, there is little emphasis on how to develop and maintain an effective "diet of the brain". This may sound like the selection of "superfoods" that increase cognitive abilities – and there may be some truth there. What I am recommending here, however, is a dedicated and effective mind-training programme. It is a glaring omission, considering just how pivotal the thought muscle is to just about everything we do. We are often not taught how our overall health, well-being, and behaviours are deeply impacted by our ability to observe our mind and our thoughts.

Recently, a friend was telling me about a male acquaintance who devotes his time and much of his money to being among the fittest specimens of the human race. He surfs and works out regularly and has the ripped muscles and bulging biceps to prove it, but he does not know how to get his career off the ground. He seems to continually be locked in the same "failing relationship" he is terrible with money management and is unable to come up with new ideas for his business. He has a six-pack and most of his fibrous tissues are finely-honed, but the one muscle that is not being worked is the one that drives the others.

I believe in the philosophical viewpoint that if we concentrate on our thoughts, our thoughts become our habits, our habits become our behaviour and our behaviour becomes our destiny. Even if you do not follow the same thinking, scientifically, how we think is how we experience reality. As human beings, our eyes move at a rapid speed and the brain acts to artificially stabilise the eyes. Information from the eyes passes through the visual cortex into the brain, with a delay, so we do not actually experience visual reality in real time. During that delay, we cross-match what we have just experienced with our internal story.

Reality is purely a perception on an individual basis that is centred on how we think, to such an extent that there is not *any* amount of physical activity we could do that could compete with the importance of regular rigorous mental exercise. Put another way, the importance of maintaining and improving our thought processes eclipses the volume of healthy food we should eat.

This is not to down-play physical well-being. There is a clear need for a movement towards a holistic approach that can take into account our physical and mental health in a single view. If we look around the services for how we think, most brain-training apps are based on memory or solving puzzles. There is almost no material available that seeks to query how we think and point out biases that seem to be apparent. Indeed, it was the shocking absence of such material that led me to write this book.

This is an expensive omission when business meetings are taking place with the participants thinking in the same way as they and their predecessors have thought for the past two decades and are making decisions in real time that are the same choices that they are making time and time again, without realization, awareness and enlightenment. Businesses then wonder why everything seems to happen in exactly the same cycles and why they cannot break out of their circumstances.

What is happening is that, without an effective diet of the brain, such organizations and the leaders running them have become prisoners of their own thoughts. Viktor Frankl famously stated that there is a gap between stimulus and response and that in that gap lies our growth and our freedom. This concept dates back all the way to Plato's cave and the many writings that have been generated over the past 2,500 years but it remains highly-relevant and super-powerful in terms of Advanced Thought.

The three critical factors that enable us to respond effectively to thoughts and other stimulus are pausing, obtaining clarity and making choices. We experience stimulus in guises ranging from our alarm clocks ringing in the mornings, our buses being late, the boss treating us badly or the company's shareholders increasing pressure on the executives. Any form of stimulus tends to trigger a neurological reaction inside of us that uses the same pattern as it did in the past to react. If you tend to get angry and your blood pressure rises when your bus is late, that is increasingly what happens when the bus continues not to arrive. We live inside that pattern, which is my starting point for defining a lack of response, which is basically a reaction that simply re-enacts a pattern. About 90 per cent of the estimated 60,000-70,000 thoughts that we have each day are the very same thoughts that we entertained the day before.

Those repeated thoughts are driving reactions that literally produce the same reality as the past. We are therefore marching headlong into the future using the rear-view mirror as a navigation system. This is why new stimulus can have a startling effect, but it is also a reason why human beings are so resistant to change. A very big part of it is that we generate an extraordinary comfort from doing the same things again and again, while expecting a different result – a behaviour that Einstein classed as insanity. Many of us are effectively sleepwalking our way through our lives.

Neurones that fire together are wired together so the biological reaction of the human brain to thinking the same thoughts several times is to form a path. The Pavlovian dog that learns from its master's voice on the phonographic turntable is actually just a neurological system that maps cause and effect. It is not just dogs that are affected in this way. In humans, neuro-linguistic programming is one of the most popular frameworks for rewiring such frameworks. It is also a key part of hypnotherapy. This is the power of thought, whether it is achieved through words, music or magnets.

The pure scientific truth is that our body does not know the difference between an experience like this, or a drug that it is taking, and the thought of that experience or drug. If we think we are high on a drug, our bodies change their cellular infrastructure to be high on that drug. In scientific tests, there is absolutely no difference between thought-created responses and ones that have been created by experiences.

I utilized this truth in one of my coin flip challenges, imagining that I was physically consuming four "virtual" double espressos before entering the Jiu-Jitsu ring. This may sound ridiculous, but I truly found that this exercise produced the same stimulus as would have been available in the drink itself. I immediately felt super-charged – and I do not even drink coffee regularly. This scientific truth represents the most profound reality about thoughts. It is literally the power of mind over matter and this can now be proven. If we accept that to be the case, the predominant activity we should be doing is examining our thoughts.

So how do we go about making proper decisions about amazing goals. Our response to stimuli can be defined in this context as a considered choice of thought, based on the formation of clarity of what we are thinking, how we are thinking and why we are thinking that requires a pause between a stimulus and a resultant decision.

Its three constituents are therefore **pause, clarity** and **choice** but it is the clarity of our thoughts after the pause and just before the choice that offers the most scope for self-improvement.

Taking a Pause for Reflection

We are all familiar with the concept that decisions, whether by juries, football referees or individual minds, need time and it is customary for some time to be granted. However, it is what happens in the brain during that pause that really determines the quality of our thoughts. It is very rare that an important decision needs to be made within 30 seconds. Mostly, a lot more time is available. Thought coaches encourage us not to send email or text replies when we feel angry but to take time for the rage to subside and make a calmer judgement. Immediate decisions in such circumstances tend to be irrational. Pausing to identify clarity about the types of thoughts being experienced enables better decisions to be made.

The quality of the pause is important, not the length. A pause in response could be seconds, minutes or days. Our immediate reactions tend to be irrational. Taking a considered pause allows one to identify whether a thought is negative and reactive or positive and proactive. It also enables individuals to filter out biases of inevitability - "this always happens to me" or pessimism – "something always goes wrong in my life". In staff management and parenting alike, it is inadvisable to tell someone that they are in some way debilitated. Because when someone is told that, they begin to think it and when they think it, they become it. Pre-framing a situation restricts our thought possibilities. If we tell ourselves that we cannot lose weight, very little weight loss tends to occur.

Where we focus our attention is where our energy goes, where our genes start programming themselves to be. Scientific discoveries over the past few years have found that our bacteria are listening to our thoughts. So, when we think we are coming down with an illness, not only do our genes recognise the feeling but the bacteria in our bodies notices the onset of human weakness and gets a signal to attack. The result is that we end up becoming what we think. The examples I have already cited suggest that if we switched hard drugs for placebos, some recipients would scarcely notice, with their brains having already have prepared their mind for the anticipated effects of the treatment.

Our bodies do not simply listen to our thoughts; our minds are programmed by how we think but equally if we turn off or pause our thinking, we can listen to other qualities such as instinct or gut feeling. When sensors are placed on the human body, they show that such "gut" feeling does genuinely come from that area of the body. This is where the electrical signals and magnetism take place. This has been presented in peer reviewed research papers such as the 1995 volume 'Biomagnetism: Fundamental Research and Clinical Applications' (C. Baumgartner, L. Deecke, Gerhard Stroink, S.J. Williamson). In fact, the biomagnetic processes can be monitored in the brain, heart, peripheral nerve or gastrointestinal tract. In the decision-making courtrooms of our minds, our thoughts can play the roles of judge, jury, executioner, defence attorney and police officer. A pause after stimulus helps the human brain gain clarity as to what it is thinking and why, consider what biases are in play and choose its response.

No standardized system exists for measuring this process in practice although, neurologically, the electronic impulses are clearly identifiable. However, learned behaviour can produce improvements. Consider the common response of advertising agencies to sack staff rapidly after they lose contracts. This usually happens on the same day. The speed of this domino effect is a reaction, based on the supposed "logic" that the agency cannot now afford its employees and it is probably their fault. A pause, however, can enable thinking to take place from a different angle. Why was the agency fired? Was it indeed because of its staff or was it instead that it employed too few workers? Could the agency achieve better client retention if it actually increased its staffing? Or could it insure against this happening by investing more in business development so it has a broader portfolio of clients and will not be hurt so badly by a single loss. In my experience, none of these thoughts are normally given any airtime at all when contracts are ended, and advertising partners changed. It is way too rational for the industry. But taking account of such progressive or alternative thinking, enabled by a pause in the response process, can open new opportunities and more insightful decisions. A key question to ask is this: how enabling is your current thought to your overall objective?

One might expect some personality types to find this more challenging than others, though methodologies such as the Enneagram or the ridiculously binary Myers-Briggs system of categorising the entire population as introverts or extroverts, are inexact and self-limiting. Organizations spend hundreds of thousands of pounds on segmenting their populations in such ways but in my experience, this rarely produces significantly different behaviour and decisions. Myers-Briggs and similar "systems" of self-understanding tests effectively benefit from a pandemic halo effect. When assessing potential employees, recruiters are too frequently deducing their Myers-Briggs personality type and then assume that they will be a certain type of employee, with a particular strength of loyalty and a performance criteria. Hiring decisions are therefore made through a process that, viewed through an entirely rational and logical lens, has not a hope of being reliable, accurate or comprehensive. We know from *Powered By Change* that 91 per cent of business failures are based on decisions that the senior executives have made, One of those is to judge the future performance and suitability of a member of staff on a test that is apparently providing a tenable view of their personality.

The carefully-constructed, multi-layered myth of narrow and rigid personality types needs to be debunked. Our personalities are instead essentially bespoke frameworks of thought that make up our identities. They are determined by how we think, which is in turn shaped by stimuli that we encounter and our responses to those. All personalities are transitory so it should be possible for all "types" of individuals to take accountability of their thoughts and tune the thought muscle in the same way as they finesse other muscles in the gym.

Telling somebody that they are "Type A" of the human race and therefore they should think "X" and do "Y" is tantamount to ill-informed social engineering. According to Brendan O'Flaherty in the Harvard publication 'City Economics' (2009), *"race matters...because people think it matters"*. In City Economics, the suggestion is that telling somebody that they are likely to achieve an exam score, say, that is 25 per cent lower than somebody else simply because they are a different "type" of human being tends to result in exactly that consequence arising. Pausing during a response of thought certainly requires an ability to be self-observational. However, because there is nothing more important than how we think, anybody who is mentally able to pause to take accountability for their thoughts should endeavour to do so.

Developing a Clear Focus

Mostly, when there are times that people are not doing something, there is a *lack of awareness* that it is possible. In my view, lack of awareness is one of the greatest drivers of lack of adoption. If people are not aware of a choice or option, they are nowhere near taking it.

Another major reason is that individuals demonstrate a *lack of understanding* once they have become aware of something. In the context of decision-making to achieve outrageous goals, this means being aware of the need to focus on a given goal but a lack of knowledge and comprehension on how to actually go about it.

Once someone is aware of an opportunity and understands how to take it, the biggest obstacle becomes the *difficulty of following through with its achievement*. The ambition simply appears to be too onerous, involving sacrifices of time, energy and money that people are not prepared to make.

These are the three top qualities that I absolutely could not afford to adopt as I sought to make my coin flips a successful reality.

There is a lack of academic research on this subject but my anecdotal experience with thousands of people over the years is that more people are aware of the possibilities than one might think and that more people than we might think tend to bail at the last hurdle. Such a hypothesis is supported by the large number of people who say in surveys that they want to give smoking and the very low volume of individuals who actually do achieve that goal. It is not a lack of awareness that holds such people back. Somewhere down the line, it just becomes too difficult.

As a former smoker up until the year 2000, I am all too aware of the initial, seemingly-endless phase of dominant cravings but also of how to resist them. I told myself every day that those 24 hours were going to witness the worst cravings I would ever experience but the next day would be slightly better and the day after that better still. After four weeks, I was at the stage where no such cravings could chemically or biologically exist. The challenge therefore was not giving up smoking for the rest of one's life; it was to simply *manage to eschew it for those four weeks*. Before that four-week period, I identified three scenarios that were my triggers for smoking. I then made sure that I reduced or avoided those scenarios, sometimes substituting other ones. Effectively, I created my own placebo effects. When looking back now, I cannot imagine why I ever wanted to smoke in the first place.

Now, when I counsel smokers, I tell them that if they want to give up the habit forever, all they really have to do is to commit to abandoning it for 30 days. Despite that, most people are still unprepared to make the necessary sacrifices. The hurdle they are failing to conquer is generating the ability to gain a clear view of how to achieve their stated goal. If they do not have this clarity, it is unlikely they will be successful in generating the other thought qualities that they will need to meet their objective.

We so often have ambitions that we deem fanciful or above our station. That framing of something being beyond us can be fed to us through our parents, our friends and the media or it can be self-generated. We convince ourselves that we cannot possibly achieve what we dream of by manufacturing reasons and limitations. Clarity of thought can help unpick these biases.

Making a Mindful Choice

One key area of observation is mindfulness. Despite links to more esoteric theories and practices, the principles of mindfulness are precisely what I argue to be the starting point of being able to train and control the way we think. The benefits are outstanding and scientifically proven. If mindfulness is not for you, for whatever reason, then I will go into other models for gaining clarity later in this section. For now, though, here is a brief synopsis of a practice I personally have found exceptionally valuable.

One of the earliest studies on mindfulness and how it affects the brain was led by <u>Dr Richard Davidson in 2003 at the University of Wisconsin–Madison</u>. This study looked at how an eight-week mindfulness-based stress reduction course led by Jon Kabat-Zinn altered the brain and immune cells of the participants.

The participants of both the experiment group and control group were asked to assess how they felt throughout the course of study in addition to having the electrical activity in the prefrontal cortex of the brain (an area specialized for certain kinds of emotion) measured. What the researchers uncovered was twofold:

The experiment group showed increased activation in the prefrontal cortex (therefore reducing anxiety and increasing positive emotional states), whereas the control group did not.

Immediately after the eight weeks, both the experiment and control group were administered flu vaccinations. Four weeks later, researchers tested for flu antibodies in both groups and found that the individuals implementing a meditation practice after the course had far more antibodies than the participants of the control group. The mindfulness of those in this group resulted in their brains making more effective choices.

Harvard Business Review, citing this round-up of research in a post by Scientific American, reported that, through this mindfulness, brain activity is redirected from the limbic system to the prefrontal cortex - basically from the reactionary part of the brain to the rational part of the brain. This change causes us to "*change the way we react to everything,*" and enables us to rely more on our executive functioning rather than impulses.

The Scientific American post explains that MRI scans indicate that after an eight-week course of mindfulness practice, the amygdala, the brain's "fight or flight" center, appears to shrink. In this way, this primal region of the brain, which is often linked to fear and emotion, is involved in the beginning of the human body's response to stress. As the amygdala shrinks, the pre-frontal cortex, which is linked to higher order brain functions such as awareness, concentration and decision-making, gets thicker. The "functional connectivity" between these regions, determining how often they are activated together, also changes. The connection between the amygdala and the rest of the brain weakens, while links strengthen between areas associated with attention and concentration.

"The scale of these changes correlate with the number of hours of meditation practice a person has done, says Adrienne Taren, a researcher studying mindfulness at the University of Pittsburgh.

"The picture we have is that mindfulness practice increases one's ability to recruit higher order, pre-frontal cortex regions in order to down-regulate lower-order brain activity," she says. *"In other words, our more primal responses to stress seem to be superseded by more thoughtful ones."*

Looking at this from a business perspective, the benefits of mindfulness include:

- Improving Your Focus
- Awaken Deeper Creativity
- Communicating More Effectively Under Stress
- Making Failure a Positive Feeling

Arianna Huffington swears by it. The likes of Google, Microsoft and Nike are talking about it. Sir Richard Branson is also an advocate of practising it, stating that it is *"one way that many entrepreneurs choose to combat the toll wrought by round-the-clock emails, long working hours and other aspects of our accelerated business culture"*.

One example of the response process in action is Ondrej Vlcek, chief executive of computer security group Avast. I once asked him: what has changed most in complexity in your 25 years in the sector? To which he said that back then, only one or two new computer viruses were emerging each month. The company would find the antidote, put it onto a floppy disk and then post it out to subscribers, who simply had to run the disk to be protected from the newly-identified risk.

Now, he says that one million new computer viruses are being created each week, totally changing the role of a cybersecurity company. Faced with this development, Avast had a choice. It could have given up and shut down its operations. After all, how could it expect to make such bespoke floppy disks at the rate of one million every week. What the company actually decided was to pause and consider what was really going on in this area of technology. Were one million hackers devising one new virus every week or was the growth driven instead by a new generation of algorithms and smart machines? If the latter was the case, was this something that Avast could observe and create even smarter ways of preventing?

For Avast, that moment constituted the pause of clarity parts of the stage of response. After that, Vlcek created a robust infrastructure for the company that could grow dynamically in parallel with the increased volume of viruses and the expected explosion of 30 billion connected-devices over the following five years that was being brought about by the Internet of Things. Whereas some of Avast's competitors shut their doors or moved out of the cybersecurity sector altogether, this was his choice of response. The company took a view of the present and the future and decided that the real risk that it was facing was not a younger, bolder and much more voluminous army of computer hackers but the growth of artificial intelligence and the Internet of Things.

That supreme clarity then drove the group's strategy. It would no longer be a floppy disk company; it had to become an AI and Internet of Things specialist. Vlcek had a seemingly impossible choice to make. He paused, gained clarity, chose a response and now his company's AVS product is the most-used cybersecurity software in the world, with more than 400 million users. Avast is no longer in the business of producing floppy disks containing anti-virus software; it is in the business of protecting people's digital devices.

If business decision-making is to improve from the dire statistics that I referenced earlier, they need to become more mindful too, but they can only really achieve that if their board members and individual managers adopt this way of personally thinking mindfully. Companies and their boards could indeed do a lot more to encourage this development by sponsoring training and suggesting relevant reading material. However, taking control of our minds remains a personal responsibility. When we have achieved mindfulness ourselves, we are also much more effective at influencing others.

Developing a Clarity of Response: Refresh and Review

Reaching a state of **clarity of response** is the first stage in training your thought muscle to become capable of achieving ambitious or even outrageous goals that you do not think at the outset that you are capable of accomplishing. The process comprises three important stages.

Pausing allows us to take mindful time out of our day-to-day lives in which to consider what has happened, what is likely to happen next and what the best course of action is for the long-term.

Achieving clarity enables us to weigh one potential choice against others with as much knowledge as possible of the potential consequences, and the sacrifices that will have to be made along the way in order to bring the stated goal to fruition. This involves learned self-awareness and a heightened focus.

Choices can then be made most effectively with the human brain and body in a state of mindfulness, conscious of not only its immediate needs but also of what will be necessary for medium-term and long-term ambitions of change to become realizable and sustainable.

The Clarity of Response Workout

The Clarity of Response Workout that follows is not exclusively guidance on mindful meditation. There are numerous meditation tools available and by now I am sure that you have tried many of them. Instead, this workout is about decisions and the application of pausing and being observant of what is being thought.

When you commit yourself to one thing, and not another, clarity is a natural result. The word decide comes from the Latin *"decidere"*, which means *"to cut off from."* Prioritizing means to cut away other possibilities. By having your priorities straight, you avoid confusion. You will notice that what I am proposing here critically includes a pause as an incubation period, helping you reflect, detach from being "always-on", and reconnecting with the most reasonable version of yourself. So, merging mindfulness, decision-making and pause, the following is The Clarity Workout:

1: Stimulus occurs (an event happens, a piece of information is received, etc). For example, you find out that all the files you have created for a project you have worked on, have been somehow deleted from your cloud storage at work. Typically, this news would bring about instant frustration, confusion, possibly sadness and potentially a degree of anger.

2: Immediately generate pause by breathing in for five to ten seconds, holding for two seconds, then breathing out for five to ten seconds and waiting for two seconds. Repeat this whole process three times. If it is your first attempt, you may find that 5 seconds seems like a long time. Over time, you can easily achieve ten seconds or more. We breathe a lot, approximately 20,000 times a day, about 15 breaths per minute, in our so-called relaxed state. You might think that with all this practice we would be good at it. The problem is, for the most part, we have become well practiced at breathing incorrectly.

As Yogi Bhajan stated in his lecture "The Sacred Breath of Life" given on November 18, 1988 in Claremont, USA: *"Breathe at the average rate of one breath a minute. Twenty seconds to inhale, twenty seconds to hold, twenty seconds to let it go. It will clean out all illness, disease, fatigue, garbage, nonsense."* For the purposes of this workout however, we are attempting simply to insert a pause prior to our responses. So, using our example, the potential emotions are kept in check whilst the breathing pause happens instead. We don't keep trawling through the cloud storage, finding what or who is to blame; instead, we just pause and breathe.

3: After your pause, note down your thoughts on what's called the 'Thought Option Grid' which you can find at https://tinyurl.com/academyresource.

The two-by-two grid allows you to categorize options into:

- *Responsive:* I have chosen my response carefully and considered the options

- *Reactive:* I have not really considered all the options, but I just feel that I need to do or say something straightaway

- *Positive:* I feel generally good about the situation

- *Negative:* I do not feel so good about the situation

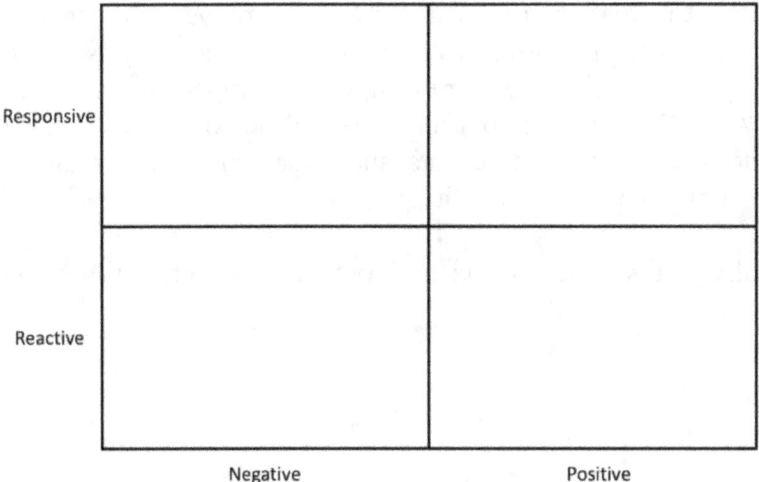

For example, a negative and reactive (lower left) thought could be to find out who deleted everything then call up the perpetrator and have a go at them. Due to the stimulus being pretty bleak (a mountain of work has been evaporated), it is unlikely to have a non-negative thought, even if you choose your response. However, if you have already done The Strength to Persist Workout (coming next), there is a far higher chance of a positive thought process. For this reason, it is a good idea to return to the exercise once all workouts have been learned.

4: Study the grid, which heuristics and/or biases seem to be at play here? Write down which of the short-list may have crept into your decision-making process. Maybe you are not so keen on a member of staff and you are biased toward suspecting him or her of being the perpetrator?

5: If you have observed one or more heuristics and/or biases, what would you adjust on the grid? For example, if you have displayed a choice-supportive bias (suspecting the person you are not so keen on), the suggested remedy is for you to consider applying an *extremely* rational question-set to your thinking, forcing yourself to uncover the real merits of the thought rather than the singular merit being that it justifies a pre-existing feeling. Perhaps list the merits of your thoughts regarding the stimuli *without using any past data or experience as justification*. For example, if each person was purely a label 'A', 'B' or 'C' without any personalities or history attached, what does the investigative data show happened, rather than the inclusion of anyone's personality?

6: Finally, activate or execute the thought on which you now have clarity.

Chapter 9: Mind Flip 2: Building Our Strength to Persist

"Strength does not come from winning. Your struggles develop your strengths. When you go through hardships and decide not to surrender, that is strength." – Arnold Schwarzenegger.

As we meet difficult hurdles or stiff challenges which require a large degree of effort to overcome, one response that I have observed we tend not to make is to persist in thinking through and around such obstacles.

Let us assume for one moment that we followed the lessons of Chapter 8 in that we have paused, gained clarity and chosen our response. It is almost certain that there then will be consequences of that response which will require us to have significant strength of thought. Otherwise, we will probably discharge our chosen response at the very first fence.

When Ondrej Vlcek chose his response to Avast's future positioning quandary by switching the company from being a floppy disk distributor to an expert in artificial intelligence and cybersecurity for the Internet of Things, he knew that almost none of the company's previous identity and operations could remain as they were. The entire business was going to have to be reinvented. That in turn required a strength of thought that could be persistent in observing the organization's challenge in artificial intelligence and using that as a mechanism to reframe what Avast stands for.

There are three parts to building such strength of thought and how this evolves over time: the itemization of the challenge being faced, an ability to grasp the growth opportunity that the challenge provides and the need to reframe the challenge so that it can be achieved. I propose here to discuss and explain all three.

Itemizing the Challenge

The purpose of this triumvirate is to first and most importantly itemize precisely what the challenge actually consists of. This part of the process is not about how facing this challenge makes one feel. It is also not about how large the challenge is, how important it is going to be and how unfortunate it is that we are facing it. All that takes place in the stage one phase of building our clarity of response and should be in robust shape by the time you are moving on to the second stage of amassing the strength to persist.

Itemizing the challenge involves breaking the task or target in hand down into its constituent parts, which is something that Vlcek achieved brilliantly at Avast. The components of the challenge that he had were artificial intelligence and the Internet of Things. Those were the problems that his company most needed to fix. The challenges were not about keeping pace with the existing floppy disk market or funding reinvestment. Those were mere aesthetics. Regardless of how dire the situation looks; we need to find what exactly is the issue. Before it can be addressed, it needs to be identified and, because such problems tend to be complex, they are best served by stripping them down to their component parts.

In the world of motor racing, the ROKit Williams Racing Formula One team recently signed a seven-year deal to use engines manufactured by Mercedes, the global automobile marquee owned by Daimler. It knew when it did so that it stood at a sizeable chance of coming last in the 2020 F1 Constructor Championships, just as it had done the previous year. Williams Grand Prix Engineering, which runs the team, has a proud history of success from its base in Oxfordshire but in more recent years it has struggled to live up to its great legacy. The motor racing company has lost its chief technical officer Paddy Lowe after first allowing him leave of absence for personal reasons. Without the backing of a global player such as Renault and Fiat-owned Ferrari or a sovereign wealth fund, such as McLaren's Bahraini major investor, it clearly also does not have as much money as the other teams.

Prior to the buy-out of Williams F1, they also had to decide whether they wanted to continue as a family-run publicly listed company or become a specialist engineering company that outsources the actual racing to others. Its other option is to follow some of its rivals in becoming a satellite operation of a much bigger group. However, initially Claire Williams, the company's deputy team principal at the time, and daughter of its founder Sir Frank Williams, made it clear that the latter is an option that would "never be palatable" for the family. Then the buy-out happened and it appeared that money could talk after all.

"To be very clear, we aren't going down that road of a B-team," she told a Netflix Formula One documentary in 2019. "Any of you that know me will know that it would be over my dead body. You will never read in the Press that Williams has turned itself into a junior team or a B-team." Essentially, then, the nuts and bolts of Williams F1's key challenge came down to the fact that its cars are simply not fast enough to win at the very top level of the sport. In making this judgement, Williams F1 has itemized its driving challenge. Everything that the group did then - and even now under new ownership - is focused on that one primary goal.

Separately, Majestic Wine Warehouses recently faced an enormous threat to its future. The company was making losses, its network of wine depots seemed sprawling unwieldy, and its "big shed" discount retailing model was not faring well in the internet age. Two clear challenges could be itemized: the general downturn of bricks and mortar retailers and the advent of increasing personalization in Western shopping habits. Its radical solution was to reverse into Naked Wines, a zippy new online wine subscription and delivery company built on the Internet with no physical stores' legacy.

The acquisition, which led to Naked Wine's management taking over the running of Majestic's entire business, not only saw Majestic untie itself from the physical retail world where it saw no future. It also gave the group a new identity as a young, friendly and personalized business custom-built to seamlessly stock the cellars of discerning wine-buyers, whilst supporting small, independent growers and vineyards. Majestic's about-turn may eventually fail if larger, customer-friendly companies such as Amazon.com move into its space. But the itemization of its challenge has won the company some breathing space and a second chance to meet its driving goal of being a sustainable operating company in an ultra-competitive wine industry.

This process works for individuals too. When I itemized the challenge in my own life at the age of 16 after 11 years of bullying and mental and physical abuse, my surprising but highly instructive discovery was that I was allowing myself to be victimized. Rather than continuing to think that my ordeal was something that was happening to me, I realized that it was something I was allowing to be inflicted on myself. That enormous self-revelation was key to me deciding to take courses of action that brought an end to the abuse. Once we have itemized the challenge, we can move on to the growth opportunity.

Grasping the Growth Opportunity

Once we have itemized the challenge, finding the growth opportunity within it is best achieved by looking at the issue through the lens of how it could be used as a springboard for advancement. Note that the emphasis moves quickly away from the matter as a problem to its potential to solve other issues. Here, the "mind flip" - or ability to control the quality of our decision-making through focusing on the quality of our thoughts - is to focus on how a problem can be turned into an opportunity to grow future success.

In my schooldays, analysing my bullying dilemma, with the realization that what was actually happening was that I was allowing myself to be victimized, the growth opportunity was working out how I could become a success through reversing that victimization. In Vlcek's example at Avast, the growth opportunity was the possibility to redesign the company's engineering, learning from artificial intelligence algorithms. Turning problems around to see growth opportunities in this way is a critical factor in making and executing the tough decisions that will make the difference in business. What it has in common with the lessons of *Powered by Change* is identifying change as a fuel for something positive, rather than as a negative threat.

Reframing the Challenge

The final part of building strength in order to persist with "impossible" challenges involves reframing the challenge as a key organizational or personal approach. At Avast, the challenge is the disruptive forces of artificial intelligence and the Internet of Things. The growth opportunity is using the maturation of those markets and technology to instruct the company's programming and engineering. The reframing exercise, meanwhile, pitches the Czech Republic former anti-virus software group as a global cybersecurity company that is predominantly addressing the threat of AI and the Internet of Things. In this way, enormous challenges that could otherwise be viewed as insurmountable have become core strategy. That constitutes strength because it is equipping the organization with new capability that it did not possess previously.

Reframing a challenge as an opportunity is similar in some ways to *Powered by Change's* concept of "elevating" an organization's core purpose by focusing on what it is really centred on, rather than the particular product or service it is generating at that point in time. In fact, every company that has correctly performed an elevation in this way has experience of reframing.

Another example is Under Armour, the US sportswear group that is responding to the sizeable challenge of being outgunned in celebrity endorsements, sponsorship tie-ups and product promotions by Nike and Adidas. Nike signed up Roger Federer, Tiger Woods and the entire North American National Basketball Association. Under

Armour was left with the two major challenges of massive market under-awareness of its brand and a significant shortfall in marketing resources, compared to its major rivals.

The growth opportunity, however, was for Under Armour to turn the tables and attack markets in which Nike and Adidas had very little brand awareness. Nike, for example, had very little awareness of its brand in the smart devices arena, where its only meaningful presence was in fuel bands. It had no market awareness of its brands among apps and very little in other apparel, other than sneakers and tops. Under Armour, in contrast, had started out with athletic inners, or cooling protective under-garments. It had amassed a fanatical following there in a market where its rivals were playing catch-up.

Leveraging that position to make a splash in adjacent markets where its main opposition was comparatively weak, did not require that much of a budget. In fact, the company identified that the budget that it did hold for that area would allow it to buy key players in that market, such as MapMyFitness, the operator of websites and apps including MapMyRUN.com, MapMyRIDE.com and MapMyWALK.com. Such acquisitions enabled Under Armour to reframe itself by turning its challenges into opportunities to achieve growth by attacking other areas where its competitors were weak. To use *Powered by Change's* terminology, the reframing has taken the elevated position that the company's core purpose is to empower athletes everywhere.

At Microsoft, moreover, Satya Nadella looked at the company's challenges on succeeding Steve Ballmer as chief executive in 2014. The company had endured a decade of decreased value and increased competition and a weaker product than the market leaders in its area of focus, but Nadella instead focused on the growth opportunity to pivot the company's strategy, opening up its artificial intelligence operations and collaboration streams. From the problems that he inherited; he was able to reach a position where one of the leading email apps for Apple's iPhone is now a configured version of Microsoft's Outlook. He also increased investment into hitherto unproven new technologies such as Blockchain and created educational units and a Cloud storage system that anyone can use on any device. Those are now Microsoft's growth opportunities, while the company's reframing has positioned it as a company of the future, not just of an illustrious past. It is winning talent from Apple and Google and now boasts innovation leaders on its payroll who were previously plotting the company's demise at the organization's main rivals. Anyone publicly foreseeing such developments five years before Nadella was appointed would have been laughed out of Silicon Valley. Nadella, meanwhile, is now feted as a "retail products and operations" visionary and genius with creative philosophies. That is strength of thinking.

Building the Strength to Persist: Refresh and Review

Our second thought muscle property that we need to refine is consciously developing a thorough preparedness for the need to be resilient in the tough times ahead.

Itemizing the Challenge

Stripping down the target we have set for ourselves into its constituent parts allows us to see in advance exactly what is going to be required to achieve our challenge.

Grasping the Growth Opportunity

Identifying the elements of our audacious goal that will open up new avenues of trade, innovation and opportunity, effectively free up our target from being a problem and converts it into a potential golden nugget.

Reframing the Target

Re-visualizing "impossible" challenges as key organizational or personal approaches allows major challenges that could otherwise be viewed as insurmountable to become core personal or corporate strategy.

The Strength to Persist Workout

This workout is based around the concepts of observing growth opportunities and reframing, essentially a different way of looking at a situation, person, or relationship by changing its meaning. The essential idea behind reframing is that a person's point-of-view depends on the frame it is viewed in. When the frame is shifted, the meaning changes and thinking and behavior often change along with it. Imagine looking through the frame of a camera lens. The picture seen through the lens can be changed to a view that is closer or further away. By slightly changing what is seen in the camera, the picture is both viewed and experienced differently.

1: Ask yourself when was the last time that you were in a business meeting where you felt like you were experiencing déjà vu because decisions being made were identical to ones that had been made before, without any critical thought. My experience suggests that this is likely to have occurred much more recently than most companies would like to admit. Remember the definition of insanity is a condition resulting from taking the same decisions and actions in the expectation of a different outcome.

2: Go to https://tinyurl.com/academyresource and look at the 'Strength Grid'. Either draw it yourself or use a printed version. On the left-hand side of it, write down the existing challenge(s) you are facing.

Existing Challenge	Growth Opportunity	Chosen Re-Frame

3: Study each challenge carefully. Think about how the challenge could be a growth opportunity if it were to be looked at in a different way. The way I do it is to think "Yes, this challenge is tough because [insert reason] but the good news is that I can [insert something that looks like a way of growing or learning]". For example, if the challenge is "Getting ripped-off by my business partner", the growth opportunity dialogue could be "Yes, this challenge is tough because being ripped-off by my business partner has meant re-building most of what I had – but the good news is that I can now spot a weakness I have had in trusting the wrong people".

4: In the far-right column it is time to record your chosen way of re-framing what has happened. From the moment you write down the re-frame, the way you think about the challenge should now be in the words of the re-frame rather than how you worded the existing challenge. In the example from the previous point, a chosen re-frame could be "My ex-business partner and I no longer work with each other, and I am sure that we have both evolved greatly from the experience." This type of re-frame may seem unrealistic in your life (it was just an example after all). If so, choose your own version that is more aligned with how you would ascertain the growth opportunity and re-framing. Either way, the outcome is to comprehensively adjust your view of the original (and no longer existent) challenge. Give it a try.

Chapter 10: Mind Flip 3: Becoming Obsessed with Impact

"You can never have an impact on society if you have not changed yourself." – Nelson Mandela

In his early career when the Canadian-American artist Jim Carrey was struggling to establish himself as an actor and comedian, he used to daydream of success and imagine himself entertaining the world. One night in 1990, he drove his battered old Toyota to the top of a hill. While sitting there, broke, looking down over the city and dreaming of his future, he wrote himself a cheque for $10m, specifying in the notation line that the sum was "for acting services rendered" and dated it at Thanksgiving 1995. Five years later, days before 1995's Thanksgiving, he discovered that he was going to make $10m for his role in the movie Dumb and Dumber.

This was far from a coincidence. Within that five-year period, every action that Carrey had taken, every decision made, every thought that he allowed to direct his career, was directly linked to the visual, tactile $10m cheque that he had written to himself. Commentators call this the "law of attraction". It runs as follows: "If you are always thinking about what you want, you will attract more of it."

The same principle led Barack Obama to head for the door at a 1997 bachelor party he was attending in Berkshire, England, as soon as a strippergram arrived. Obama was already a senator and had his mind set on becoming president, which, of course, he achieved with his inauguration 11 years later. With that target at the front of his mind, there was no way that he was going to stay in that room, vulnerable to the camera of a passing paparazzi photographer. When you become mentally committed to achieving a goal, becoming obsessed with how events and behaviour will affect the likelihood of that goal being achieved is a vital part of the brain machinery that will lead to its accomplishment.

Anyone who has successfully lost weight or trained for a marathon, climbing a mountain or another feat of human endurance knows that keeping one's mind firmly on the goal is of paramount importance. It is what stops us eating that dessert or having a sneaky drink. We don't do those things because we know that the momentary pleasure they will give will soon dissipate and that our fall from grace in this regard will damage our ultimate ambition. This is obsession with impact: a steely determination that will not allow even slight indiscretions because they might stop us achieving what we have decided we are all about.

Visualizing your goals

Training the mind in this way can be through a kind of mental rehearsal, a visualization of the future or through using some other powerful imagery that pictures a given accomplishment or achievement. Such a mental rehearsal requires us to take our own perspective or view and imagine completing the required skill or outcome perfectly, whilst ensuring that we visualize the complete scenario, complete with the sounds, colours and movements that will be present at the time.

We tend to assess decisions we have made in business and in life generally by finding reasons to support such judgements and choices. It does not matter if such reasons are spurious or facetious or faulty; the fact remains that we want to demonstrate that we went into those decisions as cerebral beings, conscious of the choices being made. We may do this to protect our dignity, preserve our careers or boost egos. It is of little importance. I have observed, however, that we seldom link eventual outcomes to the original set of decisions that were before us. Impact in this sense is defined as the outcome of what our thoughts have been. It is highly significant because keeping in front of mind interrupts the pattern of how we normally form our thoughts. We make up reasons why they were the right things to do or attribute success to being linked to what we thought, whereas the actual decision process may be somewhat different.

Sometimes in the senior executive world, this kind of thought process can see an incoming chief executive take credit for successes even if he or she had not even started in the position at the time of such wins. This is particularly evident in the field of professional sports club management. Witness how many times Manchester United manager Ole Gunnar Solskjaer referenced decisions of Sir Alex Ferguson, his legendary predecessor in the position. In the corporate world, Dave Lewis, the former chief executive of supermarkets group Tesco often referred not to his immediate predecessor Phil Clarke but to Sir Terry Leahy, who Clarke succeeded him. The testimonials were of the prosperity generated by the company under Leahy's tenure rather than Clarke's. Such activity appears to be an attempt to associate a leader with past successful behaviour in the hope of repeating it. The problem it possesses, however, is that it can end up being little more than wishful thinking.

The truth is that most people and companies do not end up doing what they say they are going to. Their ambitions falter because they do not have the strength to persist and the ability to fix their eyes on the impact of all the decisions that they make along the way.

Jesper Brodin, chief executive of IKEA (and writer of the foreword to *Powered by Change*), is a notable exception. He does not shy away from adopting extremely ambitious goals, such as his recent pledge to make the company carbon positive and free of fossil fuels by 2030. That goal puts the group and the leader at the absolute cutting edge of the corporate sustainability movement and achieving it will be no mean feat. IKEA had a carbon footprint of 26.9 million tonnes in 2018 and the figure is still increasing as the group expands. To tackle this, Brodin is investing £2.5 billion in solar and wind energy. The company already has more than 500 wind turbines in 14 countries and almost 1 million solar panels on its shops and distribution centres as well as on the roof of Brodin's house in Sweden.

Brodin is adamant. *"Our customers will deselect us unless we are good in this regard,"* he told The Daily Telegraph newspaper. *"The only way we can exist as a business model tomorrow is to be sustainable, so it's not about how we pay the premium to do it. It's the only way we can be the low-cost company of tomorrow."*

Brodin has visualized his challenge and immediately doubled down on understanding exactly what it is and how it can be achieved. Judging by his past record, I have no doubt at all that he will be successful.

Developing an obsession with impact in this way helps us to ensure that our thoughts are driving the outcome that we have our sights firmly fixed on. One could regard this as a way of continually sense-checking decision-making to make sure that it is linked to desired outcomes. Such thinking has two enormous benefits. Firstly, we are able to correctly identify which decisions led to the required result. Secondly and more importantly, we can ensure that decisions, as they bend and fold over time, are still in line with the intended end outcome or impact. In this way, we are ensuring the credibility of impact in real time.

Basically, what we think, we become. So, by having a visualized impact on a goal readily in mind, we can effectively bring it forward because we get better at what we practice, and we tend to arrive at where we have focused our energy. The old adage that achievements can be accomplished by asserting the primacy of "mind over matter" rings absolutely true here.

Dr Joe Dispenza's mental health research is a game-changer in the way that we need to marshal, police and control our thoughts in order to determine a set objective.

He states in "You Are the Placebo" that he "*set out to explore the idea that it is possible for people to heal themselves of all sorts of conditions (even those considered incurable) without drugs or surgery — through thought alone. After all, the power of belief is so strong that drug companies routinely use double- and triple-blind, placebo-controlled studies to test new drugs because people taking placebos (inert substances like sugar pills), thinking they may be taking an active drug, often improve".*

If we are the placebo then we can become our own faith-healers, not because of some miraculous or religious intervention, but through the power of our own minds. With no disrespect whatsoever to organized religion, tarot card-readers or spiritual mediums, the will that the human mind is capable of asserting can have a directly traceable impact on the object of its attention being realized or achieved.

I want to be quite clear here that I am *not in any way* seeking to deny or minimize the power of prayer or religious belief. I am agnostic as to the issue, whilst fully respecting the opinions and lifestyles of those who hold strongly to them. All I am doing here is pointing out the neurological processes that my research has found the brain to be capable of on its own.

There are outrageous but true examples of people who have practiced playing a musical instrument, without actually having the said instrument with them. They practice playing the instrument in their head and then notice that their performance has improved when they next play the piece complete with the instrument they want to make sounds and music with.

This principle can have negative consequences too. In one true story, documented in medical literature, a man died shortly after hearing that he had incurable cancer. His autopsy later proved that he had been misdiagnosed and was in fact perfectly healthy. In another case, a woman suffering from long-term depression saw the malaise lift so dramatically during an antidepressant drug trial that she was sure she was receiving the active drug. In actual fact, however, she was part of the placebo group. When she was told this, she suffered a relapse. In a third case, a handful of veterans severely hobbled by osteoarthritis regained pain-free mobility after a surgeon performed sham surgery, making small incisions in their knees and then sewing them back up without doing anything else. While the surgery was fake and non-existent, the recoveries were real enough.

Equally, if we do not think about the consequences of our decisions before we make them, the chances of them being favourable to our goals are literally random.

In the film Kumaré, an American documentary-maker set out to test whether faith-healing actually works. He invented a fictitious character, an Indian faith-healer whose name is the title of the movie, and toured the US pretending to be him, with fascinating results. In one scene, he asks people to visualize a blue light. He asks if they can see a blue light and all his respondents magically can. He then asks them to focus on the light and as they do, their lives instantly become more fulfilling, happy and healthy. As he travels the country, the people he affects have no idea that they are part of a filmed documentary setting out to demonstrate the power of thought. At the film's end, he announces to a crowd of devotees that his name is not Kumaré and he does not descend from the lineage of faith-healing that he had purported to be true. He tells them that he is instead a film-maker who has only been to India once but, amazingly, the majority of his following tell him, unabashed, that he has still changed their lives.

Cases like this would seem to support Dispenza's main premise. *"When you imagine a desired outcome, by doing so you make your inner thoughts more real than your outer environment. If you combine a clear intention of the new future that you want with an elevated emotion, such as joy and gratitude, you can give your body a taste of this future experience in the present moment. If you make it feel real enough, your brain will not know the difference and will fire new neurons and make new connections until it starts to look as if the event has actually taken place. Our body does not know the difference between an experience that creates an emotion versus an emotion created by thought alone. Bearing that in mind, it is also true that our environment of experience signals our genes to switch elements on or off and all genes make proteins. Proteins are responsible for the structure and function of our body so therefore once we think, our body begins to change into the future state we are thinking about."*

Becoming Obsessed with Impact: Refresh and Review

Visualizing our goal in glorious technicolour detail can act as a powerful tool as we put ourselves through the tortuous training and preparation aimed at helping us to achieve it.

An unyielding commitment to reaching this vision of nirvana provides us with a method of continually sense-checking all of our decision-making to absolutely ensure that it is linked to desired outcomes. If it is not; it simply can not and does not happen.

Such thinking helps us to correctly identify which decisions led to our required result and means that as decisions change over time, we can make sure that they are on track to get us over the finish line.

The Impact Workout: The Seven Steps to Positively Impacting Your Goals

The following plan is what has enabled me to successfully execute every single one of the coin flip objectives that I have set for myself over the past 14 years – despite being absolutely convinced at the time of goal-setting that I was not capable of doing so. I have also used it for career-related goals, and it has worked equally well. I share it with you here with one condition attached. In order for your desired outcome to be realized, you have to enter the process convinced that you do have the ability to affect the impact of what you do and that your thoughts can have the impact that you desire. If you do not believe this, I can guarantee that it will not happen.

Remember that life is just as much about the journey you take to reach your goals as it is about the destination you have in mind. Visualization can make the process of reaching your goal more enjoyable by keeping you focused and motivated, making it a positive addition to your life. I have tried dozens of different approaches and have created my own version which is extremely effective. I hope you find it of value.

Step One: Visualize the Activity, Event, or Result that you Desire

Find a super-quiet space, somewhere well away from others. Close your eyes and visualize exactly what you really want to achieve, not simply as a vague big-picture ambition, but in granular detail. If you have a desire for your company to "make a difference," think precisely about who will feel that difference. How will it affect associates, employees, customers, communities, the talented, the under-privileged, your peers, your family and yourself? Exactly what will it look, feel and be like? What will it include? What will be its limits? If you are visualizing your organization expanding into South America, specify where you want the head office to be, how many floors it will have and how many people will work there. Think about how long it will take to build it and what that will cost. What will your branding look like at the reception desk there?

Such a detailed level of granularity is essential to this first exercise because we tend to think in generalities or even platitudes. When I ask a restaurant owner how he or she visualizes further success, they invariably answer that they would like to have more restaurants. For their plans to have the impact that they desire, they need to be deciding how many restaurants they need, where they need to be, what types of staff and customers they will have and what type of food they will serve. There is no actual upward limit to how granular this can be. You can go as far as to imagine in this example on what days the new outlets will be open, what they will look like, who will want to eat there, how many customers they will service and how much money they will make. Choose the wallpaper or table effects in advance if that is what it takes. The key is to know exactly what you are setting out to achieve.

Step Two: Create Visual Imagery Connected to your Goal

This can be a vision board, a notebook, a picture, photomontage, Pinterest or Instagram account, private photograph album or all of the above. What is important is that it provides actual visual imagery that supports exactly what your visualized mental rehearsal looks like. This will help you visualize your goals on a regular basis. To make a vision board, post a collection of photos and words that represent your future goals. That way, you can look at them every day to stay motivated and be reminded of why you are doing what you are doing. If your goal is to become the chief executive of a large organization, find some photos of the coolest office you can find. What is in the room, other than yourself, of course? What is on the floor and on the walls? How comfy is the corner sofa? What is the view from the window? Picture all this, capture it and put it somewhere safe so you can track your progress towards this goal.

For Jim Carrey, this step involved physically writing out a cheque for $10m, marked for cashing to himself in five years' time. He could have simply written down that he wanted to become famous and rich but the granularity and specificity of his goals and the way that he created an actual, physical visualization of them helped him focus on every single day of the next 60 months on achieving precisely that outcome. Staring every day at your vision board, notebook or whatever shape your visual memory takes will enable you to stay motivated and to remain mindful of what it is that you are really heading out to seek to achieve.

Step Three. Consider the Actual Chain of Events Needed to Achieve Your Goal

Major changes in your life take large amounts of time, energy and personal focus, but actually consist of a number of small steps. If you are visualizing attaining a specific goal or end-point, imagine precisely how you plan to get there. If you want to be a leader of a certain organization or start your own global charity, what are the actual critical actions that you need to be taking now, tomorrow, the day after that and in the weeks and months that follow?

If your goal is to open five restaurants in London, there are locations to be chosen, licences to be applied for and granted, financing to be put in place, interior design to be decided upon, menus to be drawn up and many other decisions. What are the actual steps needed and in what order do they need to happen? Once you have determined exactly what these stages are, you need to order them in a way that makes logical sense, even if they still feel distant or difficult to achieve. Itemizing the chain of events necessary to achieve your goal will directly increase your chances of doing so. Remember again that this is not wishful thinking, and the chain of events needs to be full of steps that you can control. This is not about waiting for an inheritance or a lottery win. These itemized and timed steps need to be actionable directly by yourself.

Step Four: Start to Move Your Visualization into the Real World Around You

Begin to make changes in your life to bring about your goal. This stage is where the magic of our process really starts and is one of my favourite steps out of the seven. Focus very clearly on the picture of the actions that you are about to take and how it is linked to what you have visualized, made a physical memory of and itemized into stages. Then start to make changes in your life or organization that will enable your goal to be realized. These can be minor changes like looking at job opportunities or something more major such as learning a new skill that is required for the visualized future reality to happen.

If you want to open a chain of sports goods retailers and have never actually done so, it would be a good idea to research and understand how this retail sector and the sports science that underpins it actually works. It would be sensible too to begin to get a grip on the main sports brands that dominate the market and how you intend to get to know them and their wares. Maybe there is a consumer research course you can undertake to teach you about sports goods buyers, who they are, how they think and how to target their custom. You need to understand sports and you also need to understand retail. There are steps that you can take to begin to do both. Making real-world changes in this way equips you with the skills you will need to achieve your targets, bringing them closer to reality. Already by step four, this seven-stage process has forced you to transform your goal from a woolly, general idea to a precise, accurate, scaled and measured plan of what you need to do to achieve it. You are on your way on that journey. Before you know it, through the chain of events that you have created and your visual representation of what the wider dream looks like, you have actually started to create the future and the present and what you think you can become. Mind is beginning to dominate matter.

Step Five: Create a Selection of Affirmative Phrases to Motivate Yourself

Pictures are fine for the vision board, but words are needed now. Establish phrases that you say out loud to yourself on a daily basis. It is extremely important that you do not merely say these words; you should find any way possible to actually believe them.

In the achievement of my coin flips, I always start by deciding whether they are actually humanly possible by anybody and whether anyone has achieved them ever before. The second part of my self-affirmation is then to say: "Well, if someone else can do this, there must be a way that I can learn how to do it too".

When setting out to achieve my goal of competing at the Jiu-Jitsu championships, I asked my trainers whether any human had ever arrived at the competition and won a medal there with just six months knowledge of the martial art. They all knew a random person who had done so. I then knew it was possible. As the process of achieving the coin flips moves forward, I step up the language. When I was training for the world championships, I regularly recited half a dozen statements, such as: "I am completely able to compete at this level". Such phrases need to be tangible at a granular level. Stating that "I feel good today" is nowhere near as powerful as saying: "I am gaining all the skills and abilities needed to achieve my target". By making the latter statement, you are codifying how you are going to do it.

Repeat these self-affirming phrases to yourself many times every day. With repetition, the phrases become more real over time and as your training and skills-learning progress, the codification increases. When training for a marathon, for example, the recommended practice is to begin by running 1.1 miles and then complete 1.2 miles the following day. After a while, the leaps between the distances become bigger. About two weeks before the race, I had got up to 20 miles. I never ran any further until the day of the event itself, but I knew that if I could run 20 miles, then I could run 26. "I can run 26 miles" became my mantra. I knew that the adrenaline and the crowd of 100,000 people would take me across the finishing line.

Step Six: Imagine Yourself Overcoming Setbacks

Obstacles are a normal part of life, and no-one reaches success without first encountering failure. This is why the Strength to Persist Workout is so necessary at this step in our quest to achieve impact. Use that strength here in this step, to know that you will make mistakes but remember that you can overcome these hurdles, reframing them into brilliant lessons. How you bounce back after a setback is more important than the fact that you made a mistake or suffered a challenge in the first place. Ask yourself daily, "What can I do today to make myself better tomorrow so that I am closer to my vision?"

When I started my marathon training, I was told that by mile ten, 12 or 14 in training, every part of my body was going to hurt. I therefore spent the first five weeks not just running longer distances each day but mentally rehearsing how I would overcome feeling such pain. When I began my language courses, there was a feeling of encouragement when I mastered the easy phrases and then dark moments when compound phrases were introduced and learning the tongues I had chosen seemed to become enormously complicated. One problem is that human beings do not tend to pay much attention or invest much time in attending to pain or suffering; our strategy is usually just to try to avoid it. But if you know in advance that you are going to suffer pain of setbacks, you can rehearse how you are going to overcome that. The way that I do that with my coin flip challenges is to consider how I could reframe these obstacles into a way of learning even more.

In my marathon training therefore, when I started feeling my Achilles tendon ache, I invested time, effort and enthusiasm in researching Achilles pain. I found that there are certain reasons for Achilles pain that I could address; the primary one being running gait, or how I was actually running. Nobody had told me that, but it was something that I could learn. Then I went to the running shop and asked what I could do about the pain and they told me that I was not using the right running shoes. That was something I could fix. I had already imagined the obstacle because I had been told that I would suffer pain. When that pain became a reality, I reframed that experience into a lesson about how to reduce that pain. And the only reason that I ended up being able to run that marathon was that it turned out that the way that I run needs certain shoes. Mind you, I still damaged my Achilles and I generally now suspect that humans are not meant to run 26.2 miles!

In a business context, let us go back to the ambition we explored earlier to open a chain of restaurants around London. One of the clearly identifiable obstacles is going to be getting alcohol licences for those premises. Apart from the finance needed to start up and pay the rent, this is likely to be the biggest difficulty we are going to face. Because we know this, however, we can prepare for it by becoming deeply knowledgeable about restaurant licences. Knowing in advance what the setbacks are likely to be in our quest to achieve our goals enables us to learn much more about those obstacles and to use them as a lesson. If you do not know about them in advance, you run a huge risk of running into them by mistake.

My maiden (and only) marathon attempt in 2006 happened to fall on the hottest day of the year. Because I was at the back of the field, by the time I got to the water stations, all the supplies had gone. In all my training runs, I had brought with me all the liquids I would need. Nobody had told me that there was a chance of running out of water on the big day. I had to then ask myself if it was possible to run for a few hours on no more water. Had anyone ever done that? I knew from watching documentaries about the Sahara, that people had done that. Other runners in my section also seemed to be managing. So, I prepared my mental mindset to run the rest of the race without liquid replenishment and just about managed it. I knew it was possible.

After setting up Amazon.com, the company's founder Jeff Bezos wrote a visionary letter to shareholders in 1997, setting out his vision to create a store that would change how people bought online every product that was possible to be purchased in this manner. However, the letter also acknowledged that the public internet was at a nascent stage and it was unclear how long it would take to get to a critical mass and what would happen in the meantime. He warned investors to take a view that many of the experiments that Amazon was going to conduct were not going to be successful and that any profits that were made were going to be reinvested back into learning more and more about the business. This was a dangerous statement for Bezos to make. When you have a visualization of future success that is not shared by your investors, then there is a strong risk that you will not carry them with you. In Bezos's case, about 60 per cent of his investors sold the shares. However, he focused on getting people around him with a similar set of visions, rather than changing his vision to suit his stakeholders and associates.

In business, I have been in circumstances with companies when I had only one month's money left to meet costs but was faced with having to pay suppliers in advance for three months' worth of stock. On the face of it, it looked like my companies were insolvent and unable to trade but I asked myself: "Is it possible that any company has ever managed to survive with only one month's money in the bank?" Yes it was, so how had they achieved it? I discovered invoice factoring services that allowed advances against future income. I also found out how to ask suppliers to defer payment because I had a temporary cashflow situation. When I created my music shop in the late 1990s, I had hardly any money whatsoever. I therefore convinced the major music suppliers to give me "sale or return" terms. They told me that they didn't operate on such terms, so I offered to pay 12 per cent more than the trade price in return for such a facility. Britain's major music suppliers agreed to this offer. Money talked, so aligning my objectives with theirs was reasonably straightforward.

This is a question I now ask myself when imagining setbacks to my stated targets and goals: "Has this ever been possible for anyone to overcome such hurdles?" If the answer is yes, then this is achievable, and I am going to achieve it.

Step Seven: Return Every Week to your Original Vision

Has your original target or vision changed? Which parts are different? What needs to be added to your visualization board to make it more accurate? Personally, I perform this step on a Sunday evening, purely because it helps set me up for the week ahead.

Review and repeat. Then test, learn and improve. Continue through all the steps as before, repeating weekly.

Chapter 11: Mind Flip 4: Gaining Flexibility to Achieve Your Goals

"Ineluctable modality of the visible: at least that if no more, thought through my eyes." James Joyce, Ulysses

When trying to explain the concept of knowledge limitations on stage or in workshops, I have often used the following statement:

- There exists 1 per cent of stuff that we know we know

- There is 1 per cent of stuff that we know that we do not know

- The remaining 98 per cent is therefore stuff that we do not know that we do not know

This is regularly met with a smile from attendees, hopefully because they resonate with the concept, but possibly because there is a common occurrence of the Semmelweis reflex, the tendency described in Chapter 2 to reject new evidence or new knowledge because it contradicts established norms, beliefs or paradigms. It is all well and good to announce that we do not know what we do not know but that does not represent a very practical way of addressing the issue. Instead, we need to essentially place our thinking into a realm of un-common thought and by doing so, enable flexibility for better decision-making.

I love the quote from Ulysses at the beginning of this chapter. It means that you cannot argue against the shape of something that you see. It is salient and ever-present. Even if it is changing, its modality and shape still remain key to itself. Things are only present if they are viewed. If we do not see them, they cease to be present.

Elevating Our Core Purpose

One aspect of the flexibility of thought that we need in order to achieve our targets mirrors the technique explained in *Powered by Change* of elevating an organization's purpose. In that context, elevation essentially involves identifying what the core activity of a company really is and distinguishing that from the shape that it has taken to meet the market specifics of a particular time and place. One of the best examples of elevation of purpose is that, while Kodak responded to the threat of the digital camera by doggedly insisting that nothing could alter its dominance in photographic film, its Japanese rival Fujifilm concluded that the market for film was going to disappear and refocused itself on its elevated purpose of providing expertise on how light affects matter. The result is that Fujifilm, with its range of Astalift skincare products, is now the world's largest maker of anti-wrinkle creams that combat some of the effects of ageing. By realizing the essence of what your organization or individual characteristics actually achieve, you can reframe targets to fit the reality of the moment.

As I wrote in *Powered by Change*: *"Elevation is the ability to go deep into the heart of what a company's purpose is truly about, in order to then raise our sights and identify the opportunities for growth."*

Such clarity has the benefit of being able to make an organization agile enough for it to take advantage of the opportunities arising from changing markets and circumstances. Elevation is effectively the non-myopic version of what it is that we do; the wider or higher perspective of the business that we are in.

In this way, one can conceptualize firefighters, for example, as not being in the business of putting out fires but the much more affirming operation of saving lives. Considering the overall benefit of whatever it is that we do as our elevated purpose changes our mindset and opens our eyes to the possibilities that already exist simply because of what it is that we actually do.

Elevation is effectively a way of describing our purpose from a wider perspective that is not limited to one particular activity. One irritation of modern times is that we have become addicted to activities and are therefore prone to making descriptions almost exclusively in terms of tasks. When we simply describe things purely as tasks, we limit our potential for innovation by imposing the boundaries of that very specific activity.

If we believe that we are in the business of selling loft ladders, for example, then that is what we are going to focus on and that is all we are going to sell. If we are in the business of mortgages, such a mindset would limit us to only ever creating better mortgages, rather than other innovative, related products.

Elevation allows us to push out, widening those boundaries, and accessing far greater opportunities. Failure to elevate is one of the biggest reasons for companies failing to survive the winds of perpetual change.

Our ability to innovate is directly proportional to our ability to elevate in this manner. In the context of flexibility of thought in order to achieve our goals, elevation is effectively vertical: the thinking of movements upwards and downwards that we could make in our sectors and industries to give us the opportunity to reframe our methods for success.

Speculating to Gain Evidence Through Experimentation

The other quality that we need to add to elevation in order to gain flexibility to achieve our goals and targets is what I would term as speculation, essentially a method of gaining factual evidence through experimentation to aid our approach. The reason that this is important is that we are conditioned to believe that in business the most comforting situation to be in is where there are numerous facts involved. Uncertainty and lack of evidence makes events in business supremely difficult to predict and therefore mitigate or guard against in advance.

The above statement may indeed be true but there is a problem with it which is this: the only way of getting to facts, where there are few readily available or discernible, comes by speculating. And facts, devoid of circumstance and context, can lead to truisms: statements and actions based on them that are true some of the time but certainly not all of it. With scientific knowledge, what should never happen is someone taking a theory or discovery and everybody thereafter accepting that it is true forever. Science can be defined as the art of breaking conventional beliefs in order to find new discoveries. That is how scientists behave, with peer-reviewed papers and a robust and thoroughness about what is accepted forms part of an orthodox lexicon. Why, then, do businesses so often behave differently, drawing on a practice or habit that has apparently succeeded for the past decade or three and concluding that it is therefore etched in stone as sacrosanct, unalterable fact? If science worked like corporate life does, society and mankind would never progress. It would not find new disease remedies or discover innovative use of chemicals or methodologies that would help solve some of earth's most pressing problems. This would simply not happen because anybody who tried to do so would be shouted down with the perceived but not updated, not regularly-tested wisdom of the past. Penicillin would be deemed a miracle cure for all ages, despite all evidence that new approaches are necessary to respond to gene mutations and the birth of new, more powerful bacteria.

With a speculation-first approach, we can start with the unknown and increasingly move towards facts by going through a period of experimentation. To increase the volume of facts we have to hand, we must increase the volume of speculating we do. We simply cannot start with facts, regardless of how desirable that state could be. Instead, we must speculate more, lighting "small fires" as we experiment so as to arrive upon predictions that can be tested to result in fact. There is no shortcut to this process and the boldness and curiosity that it requires, improves the quality of not only what we think but also of what we produce as a result.

Accepting this involves a major leap in our mindsets, which we have programmed to reach a stage of learning that is resistant to new thoughts, impulses or theories. We need to have a flexibility to speculate at the same time as the ability to elevate because if both qualities are not present at the same time, we are likely to speculate in a limited, myopic area of the business that we think we are in – an arena filled with all of our competitors.

Coming next is a resource that I envisage to be the best route to fact-based understanding through the process that I have just outlined. Your company can be the most experimental, agile firm in the world but, unless you elevate your mindset about what your business is really capable of doing, it is going to be speculative, agile and experimental in an area populated by 10,000 other rivals.

Brad Stone's book *"The Everything Store: Jeff Bezos and the Age of Amazon"* details how the Amazon.com founder not only transformed online retailing but prepared his company to compete in these two ways against an expected plethora of copycat rivals. The elevated perspective of Amazon is that anything from A to Z is to be sold via its online marketplace. That is the reason why the company's logo features the letters "A" and "Z" interlinked by a swooshing arrow. Will Amazon eventually sell food, cars, real estate and holidays? Probably, because that is how the company has been carefully constructed. Health and well-being is now a $4.2 trillion opportunity, according to the Global Wellness Institute. Do you really think that Amazon will not want to enjoy a slice of that? That is all within Jeff Bezos's master plan but the reason why his scheme is winning is because he has combined elevation and speculation to make Amazon's goals and targets so flexible.

In aiming towards such a goal, I use an illustration called 'Speculation to Fact' which you can find at https://tinyurl.com/academyresource:

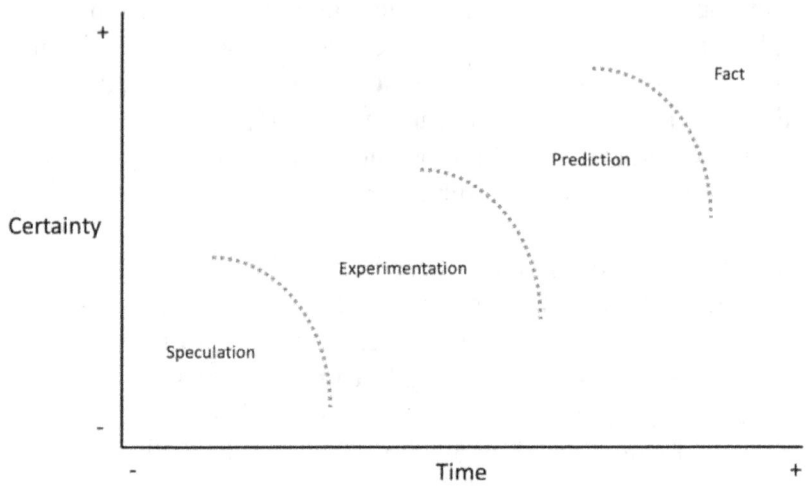

Most companies think that they need to start corporate goal-setting or new product development exercises with concrete, unarguable-against facts. However, facts change so this is not the best way to begin. Instead, we should start with speculation, suggesting possible new truths, experimenting to test these. From the results of our experiments, we can form predictions and such forecasts can then be tried and tested and wind up as accepted facts. Our certainty therefore increases over time.

When I show businesses the above diagram, it is usually the first time that the executives I am addressing have considered the possibility that they are starting their factual discovery process in the wrong place. They start with facts, rebutting junior and mid-level officers who come up with exciting new theories because all they have in their mental weaponry is an encyclopaedic view of the past. Such boards and executive committees are attempting to accelerate forwards by using the rear-view mirror as their guidance. Is it any wonder that most efforts to take organizations out of their comfort zones, and achieve goals that they do not honestly believe at the outset that they can reach, tend to crash and burn? Starting with the facts as you know them is business poison: it is the worst thing that you could possibly do.

The reason why flexibility is so important in our quest to achieve wildly ambitious goals is because we need agility not only in our elevated perspective but in our ability to play speculation as our starting point. We need to be flexible enough not to rely on facts being our place of beginning and our driving force. Facts cannot be our north star. That driving light has to be our elevated perspective of what we are and where we are going. The part of this that floors most organizations and individual leaders is that we will not know if this is indeed our north star until we actually follow it and find out where it leads. It may be that the north star is not our destination but is leading us to a better one. As we review our visualization, we need to adjust it to reflect that. All businesses need facts and certainty. Let me be clear about that. But this should not be a starting position. Over time, the insights and lessons that we learn, plus dedicated internal and external fact-checking, enable a much more dynamic and effective operation and a more balanced corporate and personal outlook.

The way that the Bill and Melinda Gates Foundation is approaching the problem of sanitation in India is a great example of flexibility of thought through elevation and speculation. The charity's elevated purpose is to enable people to have proper sanitation in toilets across rural India. Travelling around this vast nation gives one an idea of just how big, hairy and audacious this goal really is. Indeed, it is such a vast problem that even the entire wealth of the Gates's and their foundation would probably not be sufficient to fix it on its own. Their response to this conundrum was to utilise horizontal flexibility because the "facts" of the situation are currently limiting the ability of the entire world, not just that of the foundation, to innovate. The "facts" are that there is massive disease in rural India, the nation's infrastructure is not set up in a way that enables it to cope, there is no underground drainage and regional governments act as if they are powerless to do anything about the problem.

If those are the "facts" of the matter, here is the way that the Gates Foundation speculated. It asked all inventors of all drainage and plumbing globally to take part in an open competition to come up with ideas and technologies that can help fix the problem. The result was that it was being inundated with suggestions from a vast source of knowledge and experience in this area. The winner of the competition was a revolutionary system of turning waste into fresh drinking water. This is a brilliant piece of speculation that actually fixes two problems at once. Gates started the process with speculation by asking: "what if". He then moved that into expert crowdsourced experiments. Those experiments produced predictions of consequences when the system goes live, and the "facts" are now that human waste can come out as fresh water at the end of this process. There are photographs of Bill Gates drinking the water to prove it. All that is needed now to solve a global sanitation issue is money to make these machines available in every area of the world. That is just a money problem and transforming a social and scientific problem into a financial one is a major achievement.

Gaining Flexibility to Achieve Your Goals: Review and Refresh

If we are truly to achieve ambitions that we thought at the outset were impossible personally or corporately, we need to make ourselves and our organizations innately flexible, so that we can seize every opportunity to twist and turn ourselves to achieve our objective. There are two main ways of setting out to become flexible in this regard.

Elevation

Just as Fujifilm reinvented itself as an anti-ageing cream innovator to give itself a future after the collapse of the photographic films sector, we have the power to elevate our activities to another level by focusing on what is actually our core purpose. In the context of flexibility of thought in order to achieve our goals, elevation consists of thinking of movements that we could make upwards and downwards in the value chain to give us the opportunity to reframe our methods for success.

Speculation

Speculating to gain evidence through experimentation allows us to begin with what we do not know, rather than what we do know and go through a dynamic and creative process of testing various methods of getting to our objective. This type of flexibility is a vital part of our quest to achieve wildly ambitious goals, because it enables us to be agile in thought, imagination and, after experimentation and testing, strategy.

The Alignment Workout: The Five Steps To Making Your Thought Processes Flexible

1: Describe what your business does without using any of the words that you would normally use.

For example, if you are in the business of cloud-based storage for enterprise, how could you describe that without using the words: "cloud", "storage", "data", "server" and "enterprise"? Perhaps you could employ a sentence such as: "We build corporate, digital memory banks". Readers of *Powered by Change* will recognize this as your *elevated perspective*. Imagine where you could innovate as a cloud-based storage company if you are actually considering yourself to be in the business of digital memory banks.

Returning to the example I gave earlier of cybersecurity group Avast; this company is likely to end up producing our burglar alarm systems for our homes and cars and our anti-virus protection for our smart furniture. They will be the bouncers on the door of our virtual reality nightclubs. Because if they are going to truly be modern-day cybersecurity experts, they will need to widen their perspective of what security actually is in our developing world that includes virtual reality, augmented reality, and smart devices. As the group develops, its scope may also include looking after the sexual health of our animated characters. If somebody wearing augmented reality contact lenses visualizes a fight taking place with holograms, will companies like Avast also be called upon to stop that fight? As it considers its elevated purpose in our rapidly developing technological world, all these activities will become potential opportunities. Vlcek's job is to make sure that it takes advantage.

2: Consider how could you apply what you do from this elevated perspective to a different industry?

Returning to Amazon, how could it also apply its purpose of being our "Everything Store" to the world of education? What would that look like. Could Amazon end up acquiring a company like Coursera, the Californian online learning platform that has grown rapidly from its foundation in 2012 to boast more than 47 million users? If Amazon was to apply itself to education, that is one course of action that it could credibly take. What if Amazon applied its model to pharmaceutical research. How would that work?

If you are Elon Musk, founder of Tesla and chairman of its solar energy subsidiary SolarCity, how would you apply your elevated purpose of being in business to give humanity a second chance to the world of sports? Why might he do that? Because sports involve activity, which means energy. So, if you are in the business of creating new forms of energy and alternative energy sources, should you not be speculating in an area that is full of people creating energy? What would happen if Musk did exactly that? Would we get to a situation where players running on artificial grass pitches are creating kinetic energy that can power their stadium? Or would it mean using wearable devices using neuroscience and psychology to track brainwaves and bio-signals.

Applying your elevated perspective to any industry forces us into the line of speculation. We need to elevate first and speculate second. If we do this effectively, we can end up with almost boundless opportunities for innovation and growth.

3: Pick some areas in which you are going to speculate

If you were to guess at which areas of your elevated perspective could be investigated, name at least three areas in which you could speculate. Do not worry if some of them sound ridiculous or even preposterous. It may be that this is the very quality that means you would have the field to yourself and a genuine competitive advantage.

4: Hypothesize experiments you could run to test your speculation

Think about what type of experiments you could run to test your ideas for speculation in the areas that you have just named.

Returning to our Elon Musk speculation, for example, he could take a small stadium that stages a lot of matches at junior, senior and professional levels and install energy sensors under the artificial turf. That would enable him to run experiments to see whether there is any prediction for future outcomes. Visualizing experiments in this way provides a roadmap for taking your ideas from the wild and hypothetical to something that can be tested, validated and potentially brought into future use.

5: Go back to the beginning to test and adjust

The fifth and final stage of our flexibility workout is to go back to the previous four steps and adjust any of the components if the experiments in stage four are coming up with outcomes that are not remarkable but are standard, normal, predictable or boring. Such results are not going to take us out of our comfort zones and create business-changing innovations. The potential outcomes need to be ridiculously transformable but also potentially achievable.

Could a football match generate enough energy to power a village? What would be the possibilities if that became a reality? Can you imagine the repercussions of reducing the energy bill of the entire population of a city by 20 per cent by linking the games that we play to our power source? Imagine being the government that sanctions such a development, telling your constituents that you are going to help them to cut their power bill by one-fifth, just by continuing to sit down to watch sport. What would that do to your vote at general election time?

The earlier diagram traces the journey from speculation to experimentation, predictions and fact. The predictions come from the outcomes of our experiments. These can then be launched as the facts on which our future plans (going back to the beginning of this chapter) can start at square one.

I have endeavoured for years to prove that there is any other way of coming up with facts for business growth and I have yet to find one, other than accidents and fortune. Neither can be recommended as flagships on which to anchor the future plans of your organization.

Enabling our characters and businesses to become genuinely flexible by using elevation and speculation is an important fourth quality of thought process. It is not too much of a jump to state that without it, achieving outrageous goals, from coin flips to global challenges, is nigh-on impossible.

Chapter 12: Mind Flip 5: Aligning Decisions with Core Values

"When you achieve complete congruence between your values and your goals, like a hand in a glove, you feel strong, happy, healthy, and fully integrated as a person. You develop a kind of courage that makes you completely unafraid to make decisions and take action. Your whole life improves when you begin living your life by the values that you most admire." - Brian Tracy

Alignment is about enabling the link between how we think and what we stand for. Our values are important because they help us to grow and develop. They help us to create the future we want to experience. In our work and personal life, we spend a great deal of time being very busy, but sometimes we pay less attention to whether those activities are actually aligned to our values. I believe it is very important to make sure we are executing on the *right* projects and initiatives. By "right" I mean activities that are aligned to our values. Otherwise, we may be getting things done that do not support our vision nor help in reaching our desired destination.

Over the years, I have taken an interest in how some of the world's leading philosophers throughout history have approached a definition of humanity. For Freud, it was centered around man's relentless pursuit of pleasure. American philosopher Mortimer Adler adapted this to center on man's relentless pursuit of power. In addition to Freud's pleasure principle, he applied Adler's power principle. Viktor Frankl, meanwhile, eschewed both in favour of a higher pursuit of meaning. I subscribe to the latter view. A quest for meaning is the objective of man's pursuits. If we wish to lead a happy and fulfilled life, the pursuit of meaning is the most efficient route of achieving it.

If that is true, then the framework that Frankl put forward was that it is important to maintain the ownership or sovereignty of our thoughts, so as to choose our response and realize that our thoughts are not our prison walls. In *Man's Search for Meaning*, Frankl makes it abundantly clear. "Prison bars imagined are no less solid steel," he writes, asserting that our thoughts are just as capable as metal bars at keeping us imprisoned. He argues that we can choose to escape this prison by realizing the meaning of everything that we do and choosing our response, based on that meaning.

I would like to add further to this body of thought by exploring exactly how we go about doing that. Frankl offers exercises to pursue meaning, including titling one's own autobiography. He invites us to consider what such a tome would be called, who would feature in the acknowledgements, what would be the key events in the story and what they mean. I would like to apply a "how" to that search for meaning and the answer to that "how" is what I would like to call alignment.

Alignment can be defined as the congruence between what we hold as our truest values and how we think. It is the link between our values and our thoughts, because our thoughts then determine our actions, habits and destiny. Human beings have an ability to align our chosen thoughts to what we stand for in a way that enables three critical improvements to take place.

1: It enhances the efficiency of decision-making

Aligning our thoughts with our core values heightens the quality and efficiency of the decisions that we make. This is because we are less confused about what decisions to make, since the judgement is largely based on what is aligned to our known values.

2: It enhances our focus and motivation

Human beings have a tendency to maintain the energy to pursue tasks and goals if they find them rewarding. This enables them to invest more time and effort in them and increases the chances of such assignments and targets actually being achieved.

3: It enhances our fulfilment

When we succeed in an accomplishment or target that is in line with our core values, it improves our sense of satisfaction and enjoyment. This is because the fulfilment emanates from the connection between completion of the activity and what we actually stand for and believe in. The achievement of the task or goal therefore becomes an expression of our core individual personalities or corporate values and purpose.

Decision-making efficiency, focus and fulfilment are the three outcomes of alignment with personal or corporate values. They combine to produce an overall outcome of providing meaning to our individual lives and business objectives.

In this way, the Bill and Melinda Gates Foundation has a driving purpose of ensuring that everything it does is linked to an overarching set of values aimed at addressing large, scary global problems that restrict the ability of people to lead fulfilling lives. Projects that tackle poverty, food shortages and distribution issues, critical diseases and public health clearly fall into this category. The foundation has clear alignment with its values and its staff are efficient and decisive, focused and fulfilled as a result, despite the work itself being difficult and messy.

Such fulfilment does not need to be altruistic at its core. Patagonia, the outdoor clothing and equipment brand founded in 1973 by American Yvon Chouinard has a very strong alignment of decisions to its core values. Its activism on policies ranging from the environment to working practices, such as maternity leave, has won it a band of fervent followers and recognition as a certified "B Corporation" meeting the highest standards of verified social and environmental performance, public transparency and a legal accountability to balance profit and purpose. Yet Patagonia remains a commercial company, not a charity or pressure group. Although, it donates 1 per cent of its sales to environmental groups through the

One Percent for the Planet organization that its founder helped to form, the remainder goes to its shareholders as a private benefit corporation.

Law firm Eversheds Sutherland defines its culture and behaviour with the five values of being collaborative, creative, professional, inclusive and open. When asked in internal surveys, 100 per cent of its staff state that they understand what these values are, why they exist, what they mean and what "good performance" looks like in terms of client relationships based on them. In contrast, the focus of many law firms seems more about increasing the well-being of its partners. Making money may make the world go around but it is an objective that can be underpinned, if firms are not careful, by a value that is baseless. When most law firms talk about corporate mission, it is often a public relations stunt aimed at winning more clients. Eversheds' core mission is "helping its clients, people and communities to thrive". Chief executive Lee Ranson told me that he believes there is nothing more important at the firm than what the people inside it stand for. He ranked the firm's fees, its office locations and its ranking in relation to rivals as nowhere near as important. Such a focus differentiates the firm and is part of the reason for its rapid growth. Ironically, it also means it commands better staff loyalty, whether or not it is a top payer, and it has the ability to charge higher fees without losing customers.

Between 20 and 30 years ago, corporate values were regarded as "nice to have" but not central to an organization's effectiveness, let alone its future sustainability. In today's post-global financial crisis world, its merit and significance is undeniable. Millennials demand purpose and values of corporations in order to work there. Companies such as Unilever have demonstrated that projects and initiatives that are strongly linked to its corporate values perform better than those with a lighter connection. The impact of having a purpose that people believe in and a series of values with which they resonate is also now recognised by a wide range of organizations including Harvard Business School and authors such as John Cotter and James Heskett, whose book *"Corporate Culture and*

Performance" is a seminal volume on the subject. Despite this, many organizations have still to get this part of their business right.

Misalignment and its malcontents

It may sound obvious, but I find it alarming to discover how many people and companies have no or little alignment between what they say they prioritize and the decisions that they actually make. For example, many businesses tell me that they are committed to promoting diversity within their organizations. However, when I ask how many people of colour or disability they employ and what the gender balance is among their board or senior executives, it does not reflect their supposed commitment.

Often such a disparity comes down to money and the priorities ascribed to it but if you have a stated priority, you do have an obligation to match that with a financial commitment. Bill Gates, Warren Buffett and others have made it perfectly clear that they intend to give away the bulk of their personal worth and such pledges resonate deeply with employees, customers and other stakeholders.

Personally, I like to think that everyone who has every bought a computer with a Windows operating system is now indirectly contributing through that purchase to combating malaria. This flow of capital is in line with Gates's personal core mission to solve problems at mass scale, whether in computer or society at large. They can both be codified and matched with potential solutions. Organizing his values, priorities and actions in this way enhances his credibility, increases the trust that people and organizations bestow in him and greatly increases his personal and corporate effectiveness. It has also seen the flow of finances into the Gates coffers continue apace. Despite his regular donations to his foundation, he has retained his net worth at much the same level. Because his level of wealth is maintained, the machine can keep operating. If you ensure that your decisions are in line with your values, society will let you make as much money as you want.

Sir Richard Branson also performs well at ensuring that his personal and organizational decisions reflect his set of identified values. He has said in his many books that he likes taking risks, trying new things, changing the agenda and having fun while he is doing it. He surrounds himself with people he values and believes he can learn from and his principles have informed the way he has run his businesses, from starting Virgin Records in a phone box in London's King's Road to running Virgin Galactic and campaigning to remove plastic from the world's oceans.

This is a challenge for some of our corporations. By all accounts, the technical, algorithmic achievement of creating the system that runs Facebook was a tremendous accomplishment of an experiment for Harvard Business School students led by chief executive Mark Zuckerberg. Were his objectives to dominate advertising revenues, undertake social graph mapping of members' interests in order to be able to retail that data to brands or amass many billions of dollars in personal wealth? I would suggest that this is unlikely.

Google co-founders Larry Page and Sergey Brin are probably in the same boat. Somewhere down the line, the organizations that they created appear to have increasingly moved away from what we suppose to be their personal values, based on what they have spoken about publicly. I guess that they have felt less linked, absolutely and figuratively, to the values of their companies as time has elapsed and the misalignments between themselves and their corporate creations have grown. At Amazon.com, in contrast, Jeff Bezos is undeniably running the company along the exact same path that he outlined to his shareholders 20 years ago. He told investors that the company was going to make massive bets on unproven markets and that is essentially what the company is still doing, though the proof has increased over time.

The reaction of the leadership of oil group BP to the 2011 Deepwater Horizon disaster under chief executive Tony Hayward is a classic example of a company that demonstrated no core company or personal values at the fore of the handling of a corporate crisis. There was no alignment of any kind and when something went very, very wrong, total disaster ensued.

In contrast, some see Elon Musk as being very aligned to his values. To them, Musk is seemingly trying to enable humanity to have a second option, a plan B or C. His public relations statements may not always be wise, but his alignment may be more so. It certainly explains why he gave away the code to Tesla free of charge; one could argue that he did so because he wants people to build more alternatives to fossil fuel vehicles.

Some corporations remain unashamedly committed to increasing financial value for their shareholders, above all other objectives. *The Secrets of CEOs*, a business book by consultant Steve Tappin and business journalist Andrew Cave, has even identified a type of chief executive they call "financial value-drivers" who publicly run their organizations to such an agenda. The authors cite examples including Mick Davis, the former chief executive of Xstrata, the former mining group that is now part of Glencore and Irene Rosenberg, the chief executive of Kraft Foods and its successor organization Mondelez International.

They state: *"Financial value-drivers, the category of chief executives that is arguably most loved by the City, focus relentlessly on shareholder value. They are highly skilled at identifying value-enhancing corporate transactions or realizing value from portfolio disposals. They speak the same language as bankers, analysts and investors. They are obsessed with generating returns for the shareholder who put up capital to start or grow the business. Value generation is their mission and a single-minded focus on investor returns is how they aim to deliver it."*

The authors also quote Stephen Hester, now the chief executive of RSA Insurance Group as stating that *"conceptual statements of purpose and values can be overdone"*. *"Companies have to create value or not exist,"* he says. *"Someone will dismantle you."*

The book concludes, however, that there are risks inherent in the financial value driver model. This type of business leader, motivated mainly by financial rewards, can be difficult to retain once they become successful and independently wealthy. They also tend to recruit similarly focused individuals, leading to potential instability in the business and creating a problem for its sustainability. While the top value-driving businesses are able to develop strong value systems, they can also suffer from a lack of cohesiveness and team bonding, creating succession problems and people problems for hitherto successful organizations.

If you have alignment with both your core values and the values of the people in the outside world that you rely on for custom, work, or just the goodwill that you need to operate; then you have a winning formula. If you possess the first part of that equation but have no alignment to external values, you can still lead a really fulfilled life. It is just that it is unlikely to be a commercial one. And if you do not have alignment between your core values and your personal or commercial decisions, you can still make a sizeable amount of money, but you are unlikely to be fulfilled as a person.

Aligning your core values with your personal and business decisions will enable the foundations of your life and company to have merit. Those foundations will provide you with efficiency, focus and fulfilment. The bedrock of any activity is the congruence between what we stand for or believe in and what we think and therefore do. I believe that there is no factor that is more important for success than this, even the ability discussed in *Powered by Change* to cope with the transformation of industries, nations and the entire global economy.

If you want to be powered by change, you have to hold a value of evolution or progression. Unless these qualities are front and center in your mind, then why would you be at all interested in learning how to survive and thrive in a world brimming with perpetual change.

However, if you do want to adapt and develop so you can stay ahead of the fluctuations and turbulence all around you, you will find that the alignment described in this chapter is absolutely pivotal to being able to do so. This is yet another critical part of unlocking Advanced Thought.

Aligning Decisions with Core Goals: Refresh and Review

Identifying and understanding what constitutes our personal or corporate purpose, and which core values support and enhance it, builds a resilient framework that not only helps us make clear, rational decisions but also ensures that they are always the right ones for us.

Following and regularly updating the workout outlined below will help you identify your own unique purpose and values, against which you can track and score your objectives and decisions. If your plans do not coalesce with your stated and committed values, it is unlikely that you will achieve them. In fact, you will probably find that you do not want to accomplish them after all.

Aligning Decisions With Core Goals Workout

The following workout exercises have been found in my work with client companies to result in an enhanced efficiency of decision-making, increased focus and motivation among staff, along with an improved quality of corporate and personal fulfilment.

To ensure that we are getting the right things done, I recommend a strategic value ranking tool for each new initiative currently under consideration or already in play. This involves ranking a set of criteria to determine whether the initiative supports our vision of winning or, in contrast, will dilute our efforts, despite making us feel like we are really busy.

1: Create a values grid of nine squares

You can find an example 'Values Grid' that's been pre-populated at: https://tinyurl.com/academyresource. Create your own version of this and in each square, write down what you really value. This may take several attempts and is likely to evolve over time. To get started, try writing down your favourite qualities of the people you most admire. We can call these *imitation values*. I certainly draw inspiration from the most impressive chief executives that I have met and worked with. Another way of identifying your core values is to look inwards and consider how you make the personal decisions with which you feel most comfortable. What criteria do you use when exercising the judgements with which you feel happiest? Is that driving criteria the security of your family, the range of experiences that you enjoy, stimulation from arts of literature or something else? Note down these criteria. You will need them for this exercise.

The grid you'll find on the resources page shows what I have identified as my personal values as an example. I started by writing down qualities that I identify as important in no particular order. Health and adventure came out strongly and I realized that all of my coin flips are aimed at maximizing either of these qualities because they all required an enhanced level of mental and physical fitness.

Mindfulness	Gratitude	Health
Freedom	Peace	Acceptance
Evolution	Intuition	Adventure

Without learning how to identify and prioritize our core values, we restrict our ability to fully live a life of meaning and to take actions that carry with them a form of purpose.

2. Place the most important value in the center

Once you have filled out this grid, justify each of the remaining values in terms of how they enable your central core value. This exercise takes time but gets easier the more that you perform it – and I do recommend that you return to this exercise regularly and update it. I perform this exercise through a combination of identifying external influences and internal preferences. Personally, I have come to understand that every value that I hold exists in order to enable peace on three levels, intra-personal (me), inter-personal (us) and extra-personal (everything). Over time I have changed "enjoyment" for "acceptance" and "certainty" for "gratitude". I also previously placed personal "evolution" in the middle until I realized that my ultimate value is not to experience and enable evolution but instead for that evolution to enable peace, which is now my central identified value.

By creating a hierarchy of prioritized values, even if it is a partial one, we begin to understand what drives our decision-making. In other words, we know why we are or should be doing something when we have a full comprehension of exactly what it is that we stand for. We need to stand for things that matter in order to have a reason to exist. We are, after all, called "human beings," not "human doings". We spend a lot of time doing but very little time focused on being. To truly be, we need to understand who it is that we are actually being. In turn, to understand who we are being necessitates recognition of why we are being that quality or entity. Identifying this in the way I suggest should make our judgements simpler and easier. Frankly, if your decisions do not resonate with values on your grid, whatever options you are considering for the enhancement of your personal or professional life will not achieve that goal.

3: Score decisions against the grid

Knowing what you think you want to do does not necessarily mean that you will be able to easily determine that the things you want to do will actually serve you best. We can discover this, however, by scoring decisions against the priorities that we have identified in the values grid.

Using a decision that you are about to make or have just made, cross-match it with each of your nine values. Personally, I score my values out of a maximum score of five. For example, if I am thinking about getting involved in a new business venture, I may score it a four in terms of evolution because it would really boost my professional progress. However, it could score as a one in terms of freedom because it would trap me into a commitment to work a 60-hour week. Alternatively, if a new opportunity is with someone or a group of people who share the same value of freedom, the commitment part would not necessarily reduce the freedom score due to the alignment of values. Your grid is unlikely to contain the same values so please use your own examples. At first you can test-drive them with fictitious or actual contexts to see whether they resonate sufficiently.

Making decisions about your life, career or company becomes much quicker and easier when you have a clear alignment between how you make choices and what you have identified as your core values. However lucrative or otherwise externally attractive a job you are offered, or a corporate acquisition appears, if it does not map directly with your core values, it will not provide fulfilment.

Mapping your potential choices with your values in this way will help you achieve better alignment between your decisions and your core values. This, in turn, has a positive impact on the way that you live your life or run your company. Change becomes something to welcome, as it fuels your superpowers of Advanced Thought.

4: Turn the process back to front

Stuck for inspiration or future direction? Try thinking of circumstances or decisions that you could make that *are* based on your values grid. For example, if you have been considering setting up your own new venture but you were not quite sure which direction to go in, use your grid as the guide. True alignment lies where the new venture "ticks all the boxes" or in this case, scores as near to a five in each box as possible.

If you do not know what your next career move should be, you can generate possibilities from looking at the grid. It can be used to filter the decisions that you could make. In my case, if they do not involve adventure or health, I am not interested. Also, in researching companies that you are thinking of joining, you can check out their own core values and see if they match with your own.

5: The Superpower of Thinking Out: Communicate your values and understand the values of others

Communication of your core values will ensure that the people with whom you are in any form of relationship are aware of your values, being what you stand for. It is equally important to understand what is driving the people around you. Communication is important if you want wider stakeholders, such as the media, customers, and staff, to make decisions about you that are based on your values. They cannot do this if they do not know what those values are, but an important part of this process is to ensure that the core values that you are communicating actually carry resonance with the way that you authentically lead your life. Several years ago, a major executive preached about environmental sustainability to fellow fat cat executives at the World Economic Forum in Davos but was found out when journalists found him jumping into a gas-guzzling four-wheel-drive vehicle after he left the podium.

In order to be authentic and resonant with ourselves, we first have to figure out who we are. It still surprises me when I meet chief executives and ask them why they do what they do. They often say that they haven't been asked this question before, which I find astonishing. Very few have given me what seem to be honest, authentic answers, that seem to resonate with themselves.

When there is resonance and authenticity, it shines like a beacon. Why does Eversheds offer legal expertise on unconventional subject matter ranging from robotics and artificial intelligence to cannabis oils? Because one of its core values is creativity, which is not a quality associated with most traditional law firms. How do you know that the smoothies company Innocent Drinks is serious about its claim to be customer friendly? Because the group actively encourages customers on the labels of its products to call them up if they want a chat about anything: the berries concoction they have just consumed, a big rugby game, the weather outside or something else entirely unconnected with the company. Many companies do the opposite and make it almost impossible to contact it in a customer-friendly manner.

When we communicate our alignment frameworks, it opens a portal of understanding that can bring people into what we believe in and encourage them to do the same to us. Doing so effectively creates a new micro-universe of resonance - a new belief syntax between people and organizations. Communicating the alignment between your decisions and core values will mean that there are fewer questions about how things may be perceived, and it should also enable harmonious interactions. I have found this to be an extremely useful way of enabling a clear understanding and is something I wish that I had done far earlier in my life and career.

Conclusion:

"Think left and right and think low and think high. Oh, the thinks you can think up if only you try." – Oh the Thinks You Can Think by Dr Seuss

Five Limits

Just as I began this book by describing the five great societal problems of authenticity, digital amnesia, anxiety and decision-fatigue, reality dysmorphia and false certainty, I would like to commence the conclusion by identifying five limiting beliefs that, unless tackled, will reduce your ability to get the most out of the advice contained here.

1) The Limit of Perceived Fairness

Some people tell me after attending one of my talks that they understand the importance of response, flexibility, impact, strength, and alignment but are unable to leverage Advanced Thought because of things that have happened to them that are just not fair. As they see it, they have been dealt a bad hand in life and so they are unable to have Advanced Thought. The methodology does not work for them; their limitation of being unfairly discriminated against exempts them from ever being able to correct that situation or overcome it.

It may sound harsh to say it but the truth is that life is not fair. In fact, one could go as far as to say that fairness is actually a myth perpetuated by idealists. Thinking that things are not fair assumes some form of overarching justice and adjudication as to who gets which cards - which simply does not exist. We are all dealt with bad cards at some stage in our lives. It is not those cards themselves that limit us; it is our inability to meet and overcome the challenges that they pose.

2) The Limit of Past Experience

Other people tell me that they can not entertain Advanced Thought because a personal trauma that they have experienced in their past leaves them mentally or psychologically unable to do so. Their bad experience has created a hurdle that they simply can not and must never be expected to overcome. Society must make exceptions for such individuals because such trauma has inevitably not been their fault (see Limiting Belief 1).

However, everybody suffers trauma and there is no point comparing relative ones. We are all fighting our own personal battles and none of them exempts us from the possibility of bettering ourselves in some way. Admitting that we *could* do better in a certain regard but dismissing the possibility of doing so (because of some past trauma), ends up disadvantaging only one person: the one who is letting this trauma *prevent their full potential from being realized.*

3) The Limit of Personality Type

Another common response is: "I cannot have Advanced Thoughts because I am not that type of person." Whether they accept the binary choice of being deemed either an introvert or extrovert or allocate themselves number five, seven or nine on a personality assessment grid, their particular personalities could theoretically mean that they are not capable of Advanced Thought.

Except that they are, of course.

Contrary to what Myers-Briggs or the Enneagram authors might say, the circumstances that people find themselves in and their feelings as a result do *not* constitute their identity, let alone limit potentiality. Even if bad things happen, how you handle that situation is under *your* control. Training your thought muscle in the five exercises of clarity of response, strength, flexibility, impact and alignment will improve this ability. If you want to start with improving your clarity of response, I think you will find that this will help a lot.

4) The Limit of Personal Accountability

Many times I have heard people say: "There are so many bad things in my life. I need to deal with them first before trying to [insert the thing that the person really needs to achieve]." People use the same excuses for not losing weight or never writing the book that they know they have inside them, waiting to be authored.

Without doubt, this is the most common excuse that I hear for people declining to start the journey of becoming the best version of themselves. The version who lives in a state of Advanced Thought. It is effectively a *lack of personal accountability*. People say that they do not think that they have the time, energy, money, freedom or flexibility, relationship or postcode to be able to devote to the exercises outlined in this book. This lack of personal accountability is heartbreaking to hear because it infers that somebody else is in control of our thoughts. In fact, however, the only things that could be controlling our thoughts are the devices that we choose to use as our thoughts. If we outsource our memory banks to Google and our curiosity to an internet search and do not take sovereignty of our own thoughts, that is because we have decided, unconsciously or otherwise, that we do not need to do so – which is in itself a thought. This may benefit Google, Microsoft and others but it does not benefit ourselves.

The remedy to this powerful limiting factor is to focus on what is amazing in your life, ascribing this much more importance than whatever it is that you are fearful of. Using the Advanced Thought framework to unlock what could be wonderful in your life, business or both is far more imperative than using it to deal with the negative. Please regard Advanced Thought as an effective code to unlock whatever is limiting your progress, rather than as a session of personal therapy. You will get much more out of this book that way.

5) The Limit of Uncontrolled Thoughts

Interestingly, this is one limit that people seldom self-diagnose. The truth is that if you think that you can not achieve something, you make that goal even harder to accomplish. What is needed, but so very often absent, is a psychological diet of the brain.

Ultimately your thoughts are the prison guards of your happiness and personal fulfilment or success. You are in control of your destiny by choosing which thoughts you will allow to imprison you and which thoughts you can plan an escape from. Your thoughts are both your limits and your solutions. If that is the only learning that you take away from The Rise Of Advanced Thought, it will still be enough to get you started on this journey.

Imploring us all to cast off these limits does not mean that we are accepting that there are no victims in life. In fact, this is a very dangerous belief that leads to political extremism and exacerbates existing difficulties.

I say this not as a person of privilege but as someone who was given up, unwanted, at birth, adopted into a humble family and then physically and mentally abused during my entire education, being stabbed in both my first and last days at school. I state it as someone who had extreme difficulty fitting into traditional working environments and has seen both his businesses and relationships fail. I have been attacked, defrauded and left penniless. I think I can honestly say that I understand disadvantage. In my personal case, I chose survival as an option for 11 years until I made the choice that I was going to chase something better than that. As Viktor Frankl would say, *"Of course, there are victims in life but in almost all cases we have a choice as to how to respond."*

Being put into a situation of misfortune does not remove our ability to improve outcomes. If we have the ability to think, then we at least have the chance to amend for the better the way that we think. If we do this, not as a surrogate for other health or as a proxy for other fitness, but as a tangible existential platform for self-advancement, I think we have a chance of achieving just that, whatever our personal circumstance.

There is a difference between a prescribed medicine and a set of options. This book is not the former but is very much attempting to be the latter. Those options can be chosen individually by you, the reader, and the results will in turn be bespoke for your precise set of circumstances, unlike prescribed medicine which aims to replicate the same consequences in all those it treats.

This book offers the opposite of a one-size-fits-all solution. Take the parts that work for you and feel free to modify them to suit you better. If you think of another step, please add it on and then email me and let me know. The Rise Of Advanced Thought is not a static statement of absolute truth. It is an opinion, some parts of which could help some people. Similarly, there are other opinions that can help other people with other issues. Personally, psychotherapy has served me extremely well but so have personal fitness training and energy management. These are all things that you can apply to your life.

Truth In Our Time

Thomas Kuhn states in *The Structure of Scientific Revolutions* that we understand something to be true for a certain amount of time. It becomes a paradigm, which we later demolish and replace with a new one. We believe each paradigm to be true until we have destroyed it. The whole of science works on this basis, reinforcing held truths until it can prove that they are wrong.

The method of understanding and improving the functioning of our thought muscles in order to be able to target and achieve goals that would otherwise appear outrageous and unreachable is something I have spent years researching and developing. Is it the only way or an absolute truth that can never be challenged? I do not believe that it is. However, it has worked for me in 14 consecutive mind-flips and I continue to place my faith in it and recommend and explain it to others. It also remains the foundation on which to get the best out of *Powered by Change* and its advice on building organizations flexible and resilient enough to cope with never-ending change.

When I was taking my diploma course in neuroeconomics, I realized that the known universe about the human brain and how it thinks is very much a work in progress. There were so many times during the course when my professor said: *"And that is as far as science has got on this subject. We have no evidence beyond that."* I found that astonishing and I still do. What does that mean? Do we actually know very much at all about exactly how the brain works?

Probably not. However, I believe there are times where we can reach a new paradigm of thought. The paradigm within this book is perhaps destined to later be disproven so that society and its understanding of itself can evolve. If it turns out that the current understanding of how our minds work is naïve, relative to whatever emerges as the next explanation, I will accept that as a positive, evolutionary and revolutionary development. Until then, I believe that Advanced Thought remains an effective system for managing our thought muscle. Empirical rather than truly scientific, it is based on truths that I have discovered in myself, observed in others and corroborated in my research. Whether it will be true for you will depend on how you can challenge its precepts and modify them for your own ends. I would love to hear your views and experiences and add them to the body of expertise that I have so far assembled. I also reserve the right to totally adjust my position, based on what you tell me you have experienced.

As with the blades in *Powered by Change,* honing and perfecting every one of the five qualities of the thought muscle will enable each to work even more effectively. For example, without alignment, our elevated experimentation within the flexibility workout will be unfulfilling, regardless of the outcome. Equally, without flexibility, the optimal behaviours found within the impact workout are unlikely to result in the type of impact that matters to us.

A healthy mind and body conventionally suggests mindset and physical health whereas I have argued here that it should include a deep investigation into, and training of, our thought muscle. In a time where we have never had more distractions around us, connected with myriad technologies that compete for our attention, I believe that it is time for the thought muscle to be prioritized urgently. If we are what we think but we still do not really understand how we think, we may be at the beginning, rather than the end of this discovery process. This book contains the edges of where we currently are.

It is my hope that with these workouts and a true understanding of the patterns we fall into, we can continue to prosper, grow and evolve in ways that humankind is yet to experience.

Final Words

In 2018 I wrote a blog called 'The Real Reality'. That marked a vital moment on my journey in to how we think. It seemed fitting to re-publish it here for you:

>Starts<

I'm fascinated by the way our brains operate, generating thoughts that generate our framework of what we call reality. I first became interested with the way we think when I studied Social Biology at college many years ago. This fascination never relented.

Interestingly, it takes around half a second for something to happen and our brain then experiencing it. In that time there's a lot of processing that happens where the brain is essentially constructing a story. This story, not the thing that happened, becomes our reality.

Different for everyone and, in fact, meaning that we're all living in the past by about half a second.

Our brains have far more input on what we experience than our senses provide. For example, when we see something in front of us, there's far less traffic coming inbound to our brain than there is coming outbound from our expectations. These expectations make up what is called our "internal model".

A clear example of this is what happens when we look at something. Our eyes aren't remotely stable, they move 4 times a second. What's happening is what you can recreate by filming something with a shaky hand! But we think we're seeing things in a stable way. This is because our internal model is imagining what we're seeing. The visual cortex sends information to the thalamus and the thalamus compares those to what's coming in through the eyes. The difference between the two is sent back and updates the internal model – our reality of expectations.

This impacts everything about us, from our identity to our aspirations in life. We don't see things as they are, we see things as we are. It is tempting to assume that we get wiser, but what's happening is that our internal model is getting more established. It isn't necessarily better; it's just been modified more. Our memories change as our internal model changes over time. Memory is therefore exceptionally unreliable as it is remarkably changeable. Our continual narrative gets updated and in turn, what we remember and what we think is re-shaped dynamically due to experiences which have their own significant challenges.

This is because our human biology severely limits what we experience. We only pick up one ten trillionth of the spectrum of frequencies that are running through us. In terms of sight, this is the visual spectrum of colour – again, something that doesn't exist in the world, only in our heads. Other organisms have increased sensitivity on other parts of the spectrum, and this is scientifically down to how everything evolves.

In terms of time, our experience is not remotely linear and differs dependant on experience. Try and think of an experience, perhaps a bad one, that seemed to take ages. Or maybe a good one that went by too fast.

This time distortion happens in retrospect. It is a trick our brain plays. The memory of an experience expands the storyline and thus, the memory of something taking much longer, or shorter, appears real when we speak of it after the event. This could be 'immediately' (meaning at least half a second afterwards), or at a later date. Either way it's a retrospective story that has been biologically invented.

Scientifically, we are controlled solely by our thoughts, for better or worse.

Reality is, in fact, whatever our brain tells us it is.

>Ends<

In February 2021, a year after the Covid-19 pandemic originally took hold in the UK, I was invited to give a TEDx talk at Royal Holloway in Egham. The rollercoaster year I had just experienced led me to think very carefully about what message I wanted to deliver. Knowing that many people in my life had fallen ill and some had even passed away, my view was that the preciousness of our life cycle should be the primary element. In case it adds value to your journey, here is what I said:

>Starts<

We avoid looking at bills because we're worried about seeing how far behind we are on their payments.

We don't stand on weight scales or look in mirrors if we feel we've gained weight.

We turn off the news when the headlines make us upset.

We avoid getting an important medical test done, fearing bad results.

This is the outcome of the conflict between what our rational mind knows to be important and what our emotional mind anticipates will be painful.

There's a competition, a tension between the two parts of our operating system.

It's known as the Ostrich Effect.

Originally, the term was a way of describing how investors stuck their heads in the sand during bad market conditions. Now, from a psychological perspective, it's seen a label for any denial mechanism that we consciously or unconsciously apply in situations.

As everything is in permanent transformation, perpetual change - of which today is the slowest pace we'll ever experience, the Ostrich Effect is as popular as ever.

It's a relatively comfortable safeguard against any realities that may be considered painful.

If there were to be the "Ostrich Effects Olympics", they may play out as follows:

In fourth place, we surely need to address that the Ostrich Effect itself is named after the prevalent myth that ostriches bury their heads in the sand when faced with a dangerous situation. Contrary to that, ostriches do NOT bury their head in the sand when scared or frightened. In fact, when an ostrich senses danger and cannot run away, it will fall to the ground and remain still, attempting to blend in with the terrain. It should come as no surprise that, firstly, Ostriches don't bury their heads in the sand as they wouldn't be able to breathe(!) and, secondly, that despite the knowledge that the myth is just not true, we continue to use it as a metaphor.

In third place, finances appear to take the medal…after all, the term Ostrich Effect originated from the financial world of investments. From bill avoidance to "forgetting" to check balances and delaying payment through to denial of the existence of debt, we are world-class 'Financial Ostriches' as a race!

In second place, happiness takes silver, where examples are commonplace. Remaining unhappy, even if we are aware of the alternative, is exceptionally popular. We are programmed to believe that we shouldn't ask for too much, strive for too high greatness, or carry an elevated sense of what is possible.

As I mentioned in my 2013 TEDx talk in Portugal, we are meant to remain mediocre, addicted to the noise so much we are unable or at least unlikely to find and act on our signal.

The human examples of tolerating mediocrity include staying in a job that sucks, continuing with a course that's actually a curse, or keeping on with in a relationship that is draining our soul.

Taking relationships as an example, and marriage specifically; in the insightful report by Tracy Mccole in DivorceMag.com, the three primary reasons people stay in unhappy marriages are:

- For Our Children
- Because of Happy Memories
- Because of Fear

Mccoles' view, backed-up by Princeton University psychologist Daniel Kahneman, is that fear can be a very useful thing, as it is your brain's way of protecting you from potential hazards. But when you become immobilized by fear, things get tricky. Of course, inaction is the best friend of fear, and they love to work together to keep you from moving forward.

Fear drives what could be a metaphorically happy Ostrich head, into the proverbial sand.

However, drum roll please, the outright winner of the Ostrich Olympics would most certainly be the way we deal with our health on an overall scale – in other words, life and death.

To some extent, life and death is too obvious a winner, largely as it encompasses "being human" in general. But as I started to look deeper into how we handle the concept of the transformation of life through to its end, I realised that it deserves its place as the thing that we trick ourselves about the most. Sure, ignorance can be bliss, but it's also supremely harmful.

One piece of research I found fascinating on how the Ostrich Effect can have an impact in a workplace was from the Social Science Research Network (known now as the SSRN) in 2014 entitled "Experiencing Breast Cancer at the Workplace".

The researchers, Banerjee and Zanella studied the data of 7,000 women aged 50-64 who were working at a large, US-based organisation. They wanted to understand how likely it would be for these women to attend annual mammogram checks over the years following a colleague being diagnosed with breast cancer.

The data used over two years showed that 54 women had been diagnosed with breast cancer during that time. The company encouraged uptake of this program by automatically scheduling eligible female employees into check-up appointments. Plus, the usual barriers to getting a mammogram (cost, location, long wait times) were taken away, as the workplace was offering free mammograms that were conducted on site relatively quickly.

Banerjee and Zanella had access to detailed information about each employee's location in the workplace and used this to create a framework that outlined the various social interactions that would have likely occurred on a daily basis. As only one per cent of staff were new hires, the pool of people was relatively static.

The results they collected showed just how powerful the Ostrich Effect can be.

Around 70 per cent of women would usually have a mammogram, but following a colleague's diagnosis, they found the women were almost ten per cent less likely to take the organisation up on its free screening offer.

In an NPR podcast called The Hidden Brain, Banerjee stated:

"We find that, on average, when a woman is diagnosed with breast cancer... her immediate female coworkers reduce their propensity to have a breast screening in the year in which the diagnosis takes place. And this impact is persistent for at least two more years after the diagnosis of that woman. When women in the closest proximity to the woman who was diagnosed with breast cancer learn of this information, their willingness to screen falls the most."

So, it appears that our reluctance to face potentially negative outcomes is greater than our desire to understand our true state.

This is something Bronnie Ware realised. Bronnie is an Australian nurse who spent several years caring for patients in the last 12 weeks of their lives. She recorded the most popular regrets those patients said as they approached death:

1. I wish I'd had the courage to live a life true to myself, not the life others expected of me.

This was the most common regret of all. It suggests that many people suffer a distinct sense of unfulfillment when looking back at their lives.

2. I wish I hadn't worked so hard.

Bronnie reports this came from every male patient that she nursed. Now, our modern generations are perhaps less biased towards the 'man' going to work, so this will probably become more of a comment in females too I suspect.

3. I wish I'd had the courage to express my feelings.

What's interesting about this one is that, according to her reports, many patients developed illnesses relating to the bitterness and resentment they carried as a result of not saying how they really felt.

4. I wish I had stayed in touch with my friends.

I'm often amazed at how many of us take our friendships for granted. This isn't to say that we don't value them, but that we 'accidentally' assume the friend will 'always be there' when of course we know for a fact that one of you will go first.

5. I wish that I had let myself be happier.

This begs the question of what were those people letting themselves be if it wasn't happy? It's striking how people don't comprehend that happiness can be a choice.

In all these death bed regrets, there's evidently been a realisation of a transition, which then generates an assessment of what really matters.

This could be classed as clarity.

What I'm fascinated with is why this doesn't happen sooner?

Why does clarity tend to come when we're finally unable to deny the fact that as soon as we're born, we're dying?

Bearing in mind we are all aware of life and death, surely the realisation should be automatic?

Shouldn't it be that we become aware we're going to die so we naturally gain clarity of what really matters to us?

No.

We avoid thoughts and discussion about life and death for many reasons. They can include:

- It's seen as a bleak topic surrounded by sadness

- If we speak about it, it will bring it closer to us

- [Insert yours here - there are many to choose from!]

These are the "costs" of gaining clarity, and more often than not, the costs are seen as too expensive.

In other parts of our lives, clarity is not as straightforward. In business, for example, we can make predictions, but we never truly know what's going to happen until it does. Then we gain clarity if we're able to consciously assess what's just happened. Clarity is an outcome rather than something that's possible in advance.

Sheena Iyengar, Professor of Business at Columbia Business School, states that *"The average CEO makes 50% of their decisions in 9 minutes or less."*

From observation, I'd say this is about right. Many decisions are based on pre-set beliefs and preferences – biases – that instruct at least half of all decisions.

Sometimes intuition plays a part, other times expert advice takes a role, but never does the absolute knowledge of the future, trigger a set of questions and answers based on an absolute fact.

Not once. In any business.

Of course, you'll find it easy to observe business leaders being really certain about outcomes in advance of things happening, and maybe Bertrand Russell got it right when he said: *"The whole problem with the world is that fools and fanatics are always so sure of themselves, but wiser people so full of doubts"*.

It should come as no surprise that this has its own named bias: The Dunning–Kruger Effect.

This is a cognitive bias where lesser skilled individuals suffer from a misguided sense of superiority, mistakenly rating their ability much higher than is accurate. I'm sure we can all think of an example of this.

Conversely, in life we know for sure what's going to happen before it does. It doesn't require wisdom or intellect. It is agnostic in terms of talent, location and upbringing.

We don't need to predict what's going to happen, as the only thing we know is going to happen, is definitely going to happen.

But nonetheless, the gambles we take throughout our lives are oftentimes based on no evidence or from being in denial.

We don't tell our loved ones they matter, we don't treat ourselves like someone we care for, we don't chase our dreams and we avoid discussing 'difficult' topics.

Like this one in fact.

What we're facing is truly the ultimate transformation.

This sounds promising.

Ultimate 'anything' is usually an advertising slogan but here it's undeniable.

Our ultimate transformation is a dead cert.

No pun intended.

So how can we reduce the risk of having the types of regrets that Bronnie discovered?

If we could work that out, we could probably use the technique to avoid all other negative influences of the Ostrich Effect, right?

Well. It's really simple and it is in two parts.

- *Seek out all the information you can about how to live well and how to die well. Without fear.*

- *Pursue your life well so that you die well. Without regret.*

Such an easy two-point technique to state, but statistically very few of us will apply it.

Maybe at the time of this talk, here in early 2021 after the incredible 2020 we all had, I wonder whether it is now time to adjust that statistic?

Maybe the outcome of last year is that we have become more aware of the transformational journey we're on, and what matters to us, personally?

Maybe the penultimate transformation is our attitude to how we live and how we die? That would then provide a 'North Star' for us to live in a way that is fulfilling, loving and happy.

A navigation system toward beautiful inner peace.

If those two actions seem too large, perhaps we can zoom in to a few super practical points we can address immediately. When being confronted with a concept or other information, we could ask ourselves:

- What about this information is hard for me to hear?
- How does this information fit with what I think I already know?
- How might ignoring this information affect my decision in the long run?
- How might I include this information in a way that is productive to my thinking?

I believe these questions are all about accountability and, as a fellow human, I find them as equally tough to answer without any form of bias. It's very difficult for us to be objective, yet these questions require a "setting-aside" of how we'd normally process a question (I.E. from a standpoint of beliefs and preferences); and consider them from a deeply analytical perspective.

Then, maybe, once we have uncovered some clarity, we are faced with a few more questions:

- What am I currently doing (or not doing) that I would regret if I was on my death bed?
- How much time am I working on things that are taking away from enjoying life more fully?
- What feelings do I have that I haven't expressed?

- Who would I look back and wish I'd spent more (or less) time with?
- Which parts of my life could I adjust, regardless of fear, to enable me to be happier and more fulfilled?

You may recognise these as, essentially, the counter-questions to the death bed regrets from Bronnie Ware's research. I believe we do not need to wait until we are on our death beds to ask these questions – after all, we cannot predict what will happen to us, our friends, our family, or anyone else on the planet.

We only know one thing for sure. So why not act upon it now to ensure that we live our best possible life. There's only one of them. It's an extremely limited edition.

To paraphrase Ayn Rand from her "Ethics in Our Time" paper:

"We are free to evade reality, we are free to unfocus our minds and stumble blindly down any road we please, but not free to avoid the abyss we refuse to see."

To which I say:

Let's see it. Let's grasp it. Let's live by it. Let's die by it.

>Ends<

As an accompaniment to this text, I have created the Academy Of Advanced Thought (academyofadvancedthought.com). In the Academy is a range of insightful conversations I've had with dozens of brilliant people. In addition, there's a social community you can join where there are regular discussions, and a set of resources that can assist you. I would be delighted to see you in the Academy at some point. Alternatively, you can keep in touch with what I'm up to at jonathanmacdonald.com.

Finally, do let me know how your journey in Advanced Thought is going by emailing me at any time: me@jonathanmacdonald.com.

Appendix: My Coins Flips - A Painful Yet Rewarding History

So far, my New Year's Eve coin-flip choices have landed as follows (the result is shown in capitals - HEADS or TAILS). All the chosen objectives have so far been achieved.

2005/2006: Swim the English Channel OR run the London marathon. TAILS.

2006/07: Learn to write left-handed OR learn to speak a new language. TAILS.

2007/08: Learn to speak a new language OR get a painting in the National Portrait Gallery. HEADS.

2008/09: Start a new martial art from scratch OR learn to ride a motorbike. TAILS.

2009/10: Forgive everyone who bullied me as a child OR learn to speak a new language. HEADS.

2010/11: Lose 35kg in weight OR write a Sunday Times best-selling book. HEADS.

2011/12 Commit to weekly psychotherapy OR commit career to sorting the music industry out. HEADS.

2012/13: Become a motorcar racing champion OR learn to speak a new language. TAILS.

2013/14: Learn to write left-handed OR write a Sunday Times bestselling book. HEADS.

2014/15: Learn Kundalini yoga OR learn to cook Ayurvedic meals. HEADS.

2015/16: Do the highest skydive OR commit energy to a new tech startup. TAILS.

2016/17: Write a Sunday Times best-selling book OR learn to be a yacht captain. HEADS.

2017/18: Get selected to compete at a world championships in a martial art I have never done OR spend four months at a silent monastery. HEADS.

2018/19: Compete at world championships OR climb El Capitan without ropes. HEADS.

2019/20: Learn how to do the splits OR begin a degree in Neuroscience within the next three years. TAILS. Additional objectives set: a) Learn how to do the splits and b) Lose 10kg in weight and maintain the weight loss for three years.

2020/21: Learn to sail OR learn to be a cordon bleu master chef. HEADS.

www.ingramcontent.com/pod-product-compliance
Lightning Source LLC
Chambersburg PA
CBHW060835220526
45466CB00003B/1110